RAISING THE BAR

*"TURNING A LAW CAREER YOU HATE INTO A LIFE YOU LOVE, **IN** OR **OUT** OF THE LAW"*

ADAM J. OUELLETTE, ESQ

INLIGHTEN MEDIA

2014 Inlighten Media, Llc

Copyright © 2014 By Adam J. Ouellette, Esq

All Rights Reserved.

Published in the United States by Inlighten Media, Llc.

Printed in the United States of America.

www.InlightenMedia.com

ISBN:
Hard Cover: 978-1-941131-00-8
Paperback: 978-1-941131-01-5

This book is dedicated to every attorney, whether they love or hate the law, we can make this a better place for all involved. We can have a new and brighter future, one that respects and honors the past, but blazes a new trail of integrity and personal responsibility.

Table of Contents

INTRODUCTION
Who Am I, and Why Did I Write This Book?

In my first few years in the practice of law back in the late nineties, I quickly realized that there was something really wrong with my profession of choice. I had envisioned an amazing career of venturing into the bar as a profession, but it didn't pan out to my desires and wishes for what I hoped it would be. What I learned was that this once-honored profession was now a business, and for most attorneys I met, the world of law was about making the almighty dollar. Being brutally honest and open with our clients was eliminated to make way for greed, and doing the right thing in the client's best interest was replaced by self-interest—in attorneys' bank account totals.

Further, most every attorney I came across pointed out that they shared the hatred for the profession that I possessed. After many years battling it out in the law, I decided it was time to do something to help the profession move in a better direction, but even more than that, to be of service to and share my path to the ideal life as a lawyer with those who were looking for my message. The other reason for this book is to help those who want to find their way out of the profession but are too afraid or don't know how to start the process.

I was born in Detroit, Michigan, in 1971; then my family moved to the Fort Lauderdale, Florida, suburbs in 1977, where I continue to live today. Catholic school and church every Sunday was forced on us, and as I grew up, I resented being told I had to go somewhere boring and ritualistic, although it did give my younger sister and me some structure. After graduating from high school, I was off to a small college in West Virginia on a basketball scholarship. Since I was quite tall, playing college basketball had been one of my goals as a youngster. Davis and Elkins College and the small town surrounding it were great places to spend my college years. The people were amazing, and a friend's family lived in the town, so it was like a second family to me (and eventually for my sister, who attended the same school).

Growing up, I heard the same thing most kids hear from their parents in this country—"be a doctor or a lawyer." I must have been a good listener, so off to law school I went, moving back to South Florida after graduation. I passed the bar (luckily on the first try) and found a job with a solo attorney who had a general practice. The rush of reaching what I thought was the epitome of a childhood dream to become a lawyer quickly died off when the profession began to dishearten me daily. I was on edge most of the time, and a feeling of uneasiness set in that didn't leave me for more than a decade, due to the stress and overall disdain I had for the way things were.

I chose a varied and general practice, which included transactional work such as real estate closings, wills and trusts, and business and corporate law, but I also did some litigation work around breach of contract, condo law, foreclosures, and general disputes. I quickly found that most lawyers on the other side of the table lacked integrity, which saddened me greatly. Most weren't looking out for their clients' best interests but mainly practiced for the money.

The opposing counsel would be difficult, either just for fun or because they knew it would generate them more billable hours. Every so often I would run into what would feel like a needle in a haystack, an attorney who actually looked out for the client and wanted to work with me to solve the issues, not create more. I have seen my share of baseless lawsuits come across my desk.

I always loved the business aspects of the practice: networking, creating day-to-day operations and systems that streamlined the way we did things, and general business. I discovered that for the first fourteen years, my beliefs didn't jibe with my ideal career. So, needless to say, I spent many days with tension headaches, migraines once a month, colds and flu, as well as an irregular heartbeat condition, all due to the massive stresses of this profession and the lack of integrity I observed in it.

As a "student of life," I have had the innate desire to learn all I could about it. I love to learn, so during the past twenty-five years, I've opened my mind to personal and business growth and developmental principles from a large number of teachers. I've read thousands of books and attended my share of workshops. Along this path, I have learned much in regard to human nature, why we do what we do, and how our consciousness affects it. Despite my dislike of what my profession has become, I have been able to build a law firm and a business that runs without me, allowing me to pursue my passions. My goal is to share with you an overview of what I have learned and what has worked for me personally, as well as how I set up my law practice to thrive based upon the cornerstones of honor and integrity, which can go a long way in supporting you on your path to create your ideals in life.

- Part 1 focuses on the current issues in the profession and how it ended up where it is.
- Part 2 examines how things used to be: what it was like to practice law in the 1960s and before, from the perspective of attorneys who were there. We will jump into our time machine and live vicariously through "old times."
- Part 3 presents ideas and possibilities for your life that may be new to you. I've gathered them from twenty-five years of reading, workshops, and my twenty-plus years in the business world (including fifteen years in law).
- Part 4 pulls everything together and shows how you can integrate all the ideas to move in the direction of your own ideals in life, both in business and personally.

Since many of the ideas in this book are not part of the mainstream teachings most of us have received, I think it is important to come to them in the spirit of Zen's "beginner's mind." This means that you take on the viewpoint of a beginner, regardless of whether you have ever heard or learned the information before, and you open yourself to consider any teaching or idea from a place of nonjudgment. Some of what I present may be totally foreign to you, as it was to me at first. Honestly, I was skeptical of a lot of it due to my past "programming." I ask that you put your preconceptions and prejudices to the side for a bit and step into the realm of infinite possibility that these ideas could provide you.

In Step #1 of the Ten Steps, we delve into the framework that can assist you in unlocking your life purpose. Believe it or not, you may find that the law is not your calling, but just part of the path you have been traveling so far.

Step #2 will open you to the possibilities of living your life with total honesty and integrity in all you do. I will teach you how you don't ever have to sacrifice your honor by doing something you shouldn't for money.

Step #3 will help you connect with your true power, which comes from your intuition and your heart. You will find that living from your heart instead of your head (or ego) can assist you in creating your ideal life.

Step #4 explains the importance of your beliefs and belief systems. What you believe creates your life in all aspects, both big and small. This Step provides a framework wherein you can begin to release the limiting beliefs you now have and replace them with more empowering and ideal ones.

Step #5 will teach you how living in the present moment can transform your life. The past is gone, never to return, and the future never gets here, so why not live in this moment?

Step #6 shows how meditation and quieting your mind regularly can help you move past and release the stresses of the attorney's daily grind.

Step #7 will support you in creating some powerful intentions and goals. You will learn the visualization process that I have used to transform my life.

Step #8 outlines some powerful ways you can create balance in all areas of your life, and how you can create a rhythm for your life.

Step #9 is an exploration into emotions and feelings. We will discuss moving from resisting the emotions we judge as bad to a place where we can actually experience any emotions we create, moment to moment.

The last Step is where we bring it all together. My goal is to help you create your ideal life, and this Step provides a clear pathway for beginning your journey. Whether your ideal life is making your law practice one which is satisfying to you, or finding your true purpose in life outside of the law, this book will support you in finding your way.

Throughout this book, I will share with you how my twenty-five years of reading, learning, seminars, and life experience helped me find my true calling. Further, at the end of Part 4, you will see how you can team up with other attorneys in our nationwide mastermind group and explore the power of small groups, and why you may want to be a part of our movement to shift ourselves and the profession.

PART ONE

The Thirty-Year Downward Spiral

...the Bad, and the Ugly
CHAPTER 1

No Honor, No Integrity

Let's face it, things are pretty bad out there—hence why I left out "The Good." The law profession is as low-down as it's ever been in the history of this relatively young country. Any shred of respect those that came before us could gather has been lost. Think it is bad out there now? Think that things cannot get worse? On our current path, if we do nothing, they can and will.

The sheer number of lawyers we have is staggering. Too many lawyers and not enough legal dollars into the system has created, as we will soon discuss, a hyperlitigiousness in society. We can't even handle common courtesy anymore either. There is such a lack of basic civility that my state's bar association has resorted to asking us to enter into agreements with opposing counsel "to get along." Most of the local bar associations have also added a requirement for civility to the Oath of Admission, and the Supreme Court of Florida ruled that civility language was to be added to the oath.* Florida is a microcosm of the whole country and even worse much of the "civilized" world. If our profession can't handle simple civility

---

* http://www.floridasupremecourt.org/decisions/2011/sc11-1702.pdf

9

without being reminded, things will only continue to degrade. Is it hard to even consider that things could be worse than they are now? Attorneys are stealing from their clients, setting up Ponzi schemes, lying, cheating, and looking out for themselves to the detriment of their clients.

It is so ugly that many can no longer stand being part of the profession: I am one of them. It just got to be too much. A large majority of our profession is in it only for the money. I have interviewed quite a few lawyers over the years about their views, very few of whom actually enjoy being attorneys. Over the past thirty years, the reputation of our profession has gone from one of respect and honor in the 1960s and before to one of disdain and outright hatred.

Solutions for overcoming our current predicament are long overdue. Just take a drive through most cities nowadays, and you will find billboards covered with advertisements for personal injury attorneys. Flip on your TV any time of the day and find similar fare. To what depths have we debased and prostituted the profession for money and greed? Search the Internet for anything involving lawyers and integrity, and you'll find very little. This seems to be the norm throughout the country now, and the world as well. Something has to give, and the time has come to make some changes. I will not stand for the status quo any longer, and you shouldn't either. Change will start here, but not by changing everyone else; it will start in you and in me. I discuss how we can move toward a legal profession that is honored, revered, and ultimately respected again.

I have not enjoyed being an attorney and have given the simple reasons for my disdain. For the first twelve years of my practice, the profession had a detrimental impact on me, physically and mentally. I know many lawyers who share my feelings. Have you ever thought about why society doesn't trust or respect us anymore, and hasn't for some time? We will review the past thirty-plus years and see what went wrong.

Can We Change Things?

Some say that we are too far down the rabbit hole and just have to live with what is. Others believe we need to legislate change. What I have come to learn, though, is that to change what we see "out there," we need to look inward and begin the process of change on a personal level.

Our society as a whole has devalued our daily lives by devaluing honor and truthfulness. Personally, I will not sit by any longer without doing something about it. Society has been in a downward spiral, and our profession has played a rather large role in all of it. We have to own our huge part in the undoing of rational behavior. We have allowed others to breach agreements and commit heinous crimes without retribution or consequences. Some in our profession want to keep the current "game" going, since they capitalize on the system as it is. Our profession, as well as the court system, is based on a mode of operating that is more than outdated. The platform needs a revamp and total overhaul, not just a facelift, and the legal education system needs the same.

I want to thank you in advance for your willingness to explore the opportunity for a better future for you, your family, and our profession.

> To change a major paradigm is to change our definition of what is possible.
>
> —Mark B. Woodhouse

Our Challenges

Any attorney in the practice today is well aware of some of the challenges the profession is faced with. After some extensive research on the Internet, my own experiences in the profession, and the opportunity to speak with hundreds of my colleagues around South Florida and the country, I have compiled a list of our top issues. Until we are *fully* aware of the challenges and the reasons they happened as they did, we cannot fully know what our ideal looks like and what we need to shift in ourselves to allow the new to happen.

Things started to change for the worse around the mid-1970s. As you will see, the media's dramatization of the profession as a mystical, money-filled, and fun career piqued the interest in law school of many more young college graduates than before. The 1980s brought with them the advent of attorney advertising and the continued deluge of new attorneys into the system, which has worsened since. The top seven issues, as I see them, arose from the perfect thirty-plus-year storm of too many attorneys and greedy attitudes.

Challenge #1—A Flooded Profession (and Let's Sue Everyone)

The biggest and most profound problem is the massive number of licensed lawyers in this country. When you have an overabundance of professionals in any occupation, simple economic principles of supply and demand enter into the mix. So what do we end up with if we have too many attorneys and not enough legitimate business to go around? We end up with an absurdly litigious society overrun with an inordinate amount of baseless lawsuits. Did you know that we have more than *five* times more licensed attorneys than we did in 1960? Yet the country's population has yet to double since then.[†] If you've wondered why there is such litigiousness in our country, the wondering ends once you have seen the statistics.

"Conflict consciousness" is a phrase that describes our professional culture today. As Philip K. Howard stated in *The Collapse of the Common Good*, we have denigrated ourselves in what he calls the "lawsuit culture." It's all way out of control. It's become all about the money, and instead of a profession, it is now just a business. With websites such as www.WhoCanISue.com and www.SueEasy.com, people are encouraged to dream up lawsuits and injuries. Does this outrage you?

As an attorney involved in litigation, I have seen another tactic used by many an opposing counsel. Parties would sue everyone involved in a transaction and let the defendants battle out the liability. Typically, the plaintiff had no evidence of these extraneous defendants having done anything wrong. Then there are "nuisance" lawsuits brought just to extort money. The lawyers who file these kinds of cases know that defendants are likely to pay out simply to extricate themselves from litigation. People or corporations that find themselves faced with these suits know it is cheaper to pay than to fight. Why have we allowed such situations to occur? The sad thing is that this is just the tip of the iceberg; I could devote a whole book to the underhanded tactics that are being used today.

Challenge #2—Law School

Not only are there way too many lawyers in this country, but we have massive numbers of students in law school. Give or take, at the time of this publishing, there were somewhere close to 150,000 law

---

[†] http://www.americanbar.org/content/dam/aba/administrative/market_research/total_national_lawyer_counts_1878_2013.authcheckdam.pdf

students. The trend started in the 1980s as more and more people wanted into the profession.‡ To add insult to injury, we have continued to add more law schools to the mix. Although the number of matriculations has slightly dropped recently, it is still staggering. We will take a much deeper look at this issue in Chapter 3.

Challenge #3—Fear and Lack

"The recession"—as the media has called our economy in recent years—has caused quite a bit of fear, not just in the United States, but around the world. The lack of meaningful employment for a large number of college graduates has led many to look for alternative ways to make a living. On the flip side, many grads have decided to forego the job hunt and continue their educations, including in law school. There are a multitude of articles on the Internet that state that we have thousands of college-age kids who have become "professional students."

Despite this so-called recession, there are still plenty of people making a great living and doing it in a way that is aligned with the principles of integrity and the greater good. The "recession" has become a specter, though, because the majority of the US population has bought into the fear drummed up by the media. The more you hear something, the more you start to believe it. Negativity is unfortunately where our minds head when we live our lives based on the ego. When you start to look for the good, you'll find it.

Everything is based on your mind-set, which in turn is created by what you believe. All humans (and all living things for that matter) are energetically interconnected. As you will learn in Step #3,

---

‡ http://www.americanbar.org/content/dam/aba/administrative/
legal_education_and_admissions_to_the_bar/statistics/
enrollment_degrees_awarded.authcheckdam.pdf

quantum physics has shown this to be the case. Einstein knew this, and so did countless ancient cultures. Some dismiss this theory as metaphysical mumbo jumbo, but as you research the topic, it starts to make quite a lot of sense. The topics of consciousness and awareness will be covered in depth in Chapter 8.

Challenge #4—Job Satisfaction

It sucks to be a lawyer! I know very few who are happy to be part of the profession. When I looked at all its issues as a whole, it became clear why most of us are unhappy to put "Esq" after our names. This challenge is a huge reason why I wrote this book. I had to help others who feel the same way and have grown to really despise being a lawyer. Let's break down the reasons for the unhappiness in no particular order.

1. Career Expectations. Most of us think that when we get a law license, we will be magically transported into a life of rolling in money, creating massive change for the world, and doing great things for our clients. We start with these unrealistic ideas, so reality almost never meets our expectations. Part of the reason for our original illusions is the way lawyers are portrayed in the media (Chapter 4 discusses how the profession has been made out to be something it clearly is not).

2. Law School Debt. Doctors, lawyers, and now even undergraduate students leave school owing on mounds of loans. There comes a time when they have to start the dreaded repayment. Most lawyers coming out today have thirty-year loans, and on average have a total of $125,000 in loans! It's like having a mortgage. How many hours does

someone need to work to pay such loans every month? This can be a major reason for not being happy in the law.

3. Burnout and Compassion Fatigue. Burnout is a profession-wide issue, and so is compassion fatigue (though it is not widely spoken of). The sensitive and compassionate take a hard hit when they practice—and even in law school. The Socratic method is supposed to help get us ready for the real world, but it is used in ways that degrade and demean. Further, if you have a compassionate personality, your clients' issues do affect you. Divorce and family law and criminal law can have major impacts on these sensitive folks.

4. Lack of Balance. This is a biggie! Attorneys are workaholics: some because they have no choice, and others because they believe they have to be, just to make a living. In our culture, making the almighty dollar is more important than anything else—even our sanity.

5. Negative Public Image. Simply put, ours is the most maligned and hated profession in the world. We are the butt of most profession-related jokes, and surveys show that we are despised.[§]

6. 6. Client Expectations. Some clients feel they own us and ask us to do things that are not moral or are flat-out illegal.

This is a short list. You may have your own reasons to be unhappy as a lawyer, but we can agree that problems are widespread and real issues for anyone who chooses a law career.

[§] http://www.pewforum.org/2013/07/11/public-esteem-for-military-still-high/

Challenge #5—Addiction

The lack of job satisfaction leads many attorneys to use alcohol or drugs to offset the negativity and stress our profession is good at dealing out. Do a quick search on the Internet, and you will find hundreds and hundreds of articles on this issue. There are even continuing education classes on the topic! This problem is not limited to our profession; doctors and dentists are others in the predicament.

I believe that if you live and work in a profession that you love and adore, you won't feel the need to drown your emotions in booze or resort to harmful drugs to escape from your feelings. As a species, we have become more and more resistant to actually feeling our emotions. "Feelings" are meant to be *felt*, not resisted, as we will explore in Chapter 15.

Challenge #6—Attorneys Who Become Criminals

Over the past ten years, more and more attorneys have committed white-collar crimes and stolen from their clients. I just read an article concerning an attorney in Texas who was helping Mexican drug lords launder money in this country.** I have always wondered why people do what they do (including guys like Bernard Madoff, even though he wasn't an attorney). What goes through their minds when they make the decision to proceed with their grand schemes?

In South Florida, former attorney Scott Rothstein created an unbelievable Ponzi scheme where he stole approximately $1.2 billion from trust accounts and clients. When I was a new lawyer, my

---

** http://www.elpasotimes.com/news/ci_23235796/ep-lawyers-money-laundering-trial-begin

office was right down the hall from Rothstein and his future partner-conspirator. He had a small law office, but as the years went on, his name began to grow, and so did his influence. I asked my partner many times, "How is this guy growing his business so quickly?" When the news came out that it was all a sham, it made a lot of sense. Is it the thrill of the lavish life and expensive cars that drives this kind of criminal greed? Rothstein was living the high life with mansions and million-dollar cars and was showering his wife with jewelry, as well as having a penchant for expensive watches. He is now sitting in jail for the rest of his life. What if these folks had put this kind of effort and thought into something positive and meaningful? Wow, they could have really made a massive difference. Unfortunately, all they did was to ruin their own lives and those of thousands of others.

Challenge #7—Access to the Court Systems

As most lawyers know, access to the courts is limited to those who have sustained large damages *and* who have the ability to fund large attorney fees. Contingency-fee cases have become the norm for personal injury lawsuits and the like, but isn't there an inherent conflict of interest there? These cases should be about righting wrongs. But it has become so costly to litigate that many are shut out from doing just that. Parties to a contract usually know that the cost of pursuit for breach of agreement is overboard, so they end up not being held accountable for their actions. This is a stance taken in business as well. Instead of doing the right thing and honoring their word, businesspeople factor in the cost of a lawsuit when making decisions that they know lack integrity.

People should have honor and respect for their word and the promises they make. Without it, we crumble as a society. Without the ability to hold people accountable for their lack of integrity, we end up with the mess on our hands we have today.

Future Possibilities

> You can never change things by fighting the existing reality. To change something, build a new model that makes the old model obsolete.
>
> —Richard Buckminster Fuller

How low can we go? We are at a crossroads, not just in this country, but worldwide. The options are to keep going along the current trajectory or shift and turn in a new direction.

Currently the profession looks like this:

- A large percentage of attorneys are in it for the money.
- Unprofessionalism is at an all-time high; attorneys frequently disrespect one another.
- Opposing counsel uses stall tactics to prolong cases and make more money.
- Society reviles us.
- Clients and their best interests are not number one.
- Cases are manufactured to create money out of nothing, with total disregard for justice or the truth.
- Criminals get off on technicalities, even though they are guilty.
- A simple fender bender costs $20,000 (mostly due to attorney fees) when there are usually *no* injuries or basis for a legal case.
- Loopholes are always exploited.
- Lawyers create problems they can get paid to "solve."
- Clients are exploited for personal gain.
- The profession as a whole is dishonest.

Possibilities for a new profession include:

- Attorneys work together to resolve in their clients' interests, with fairness to all parties.
- We make decisions based on higher principles, with integrity, and for the greater good of all.
- We develop solutions to the high cost of legal work.
- We refuse to represent those who won't accept responsibility for their part in a dispute.
- We reduce the number of lawyers (many may leave the profession and connect with their life's purpose).
- We aim for less litigation and more problem solving.
- Society's viewpoint begins to change, and we rebuild their respect and honor once again.

The way we operate needs to change, and it needs to start now. I don't know about you, but I really love the possibilities I see for our collective future. I have decided to do all I can to assist in creating the ideal future. Will you join the movement?

Why We Choose the Law
CHAPTER 2

Why is the legal profession so overwhelmingly attractive to so many people? There are as many individual reasons as there are lawyers. The *why* we all go to law school is an important thing to look into. It can help us decide if we entered for a good reason or not and whether we should stay within law and create our ideals there, or whether the horizon has something else in store for us.

If you are a prospective law student (or know someone who is), please take a hard look at whether law school and becoming a lawyer is right for you. It is imperative that you do some major soul-searching on this question.

I Want to Make Money

Did you have any doubt that the top reason people go into law was *money*? Society holds a common myth that there is a lot of money in the practice of law. Is the love of money the root of all evil? Many well-established lawyers make a decent living, but as we've seen from the statistics in the last chapter, the number of newly licensed attorneys in the past ten years is enormous. Money should never be the reason to enter a profession, but in my opinion, it tops the list. However, most who choose careers just for the money won't be happy, since there is no deeper purpose than the income. From my years of working with others in business, I've seen that most humans have an innate desire to add benefit to others—to teach, to be of service—and money itself doesn't fulfill this desire in the least.

I Am Great at Arguing or Speaking

How many of you went to law school because others told you that you were a great speaker or that you were "good" at arguing? Good speaking skills are a plus, but not a reason to become a lawyer. I am a decent speaker and very good at arguing, but these attributes (if you want to call them that), do nothing for me day to day in this profession.

I Want Prestige and Power

Is a law degree power? We have the power to ruin other people financially, to send people to jail, and to make others' lives miserable with the stroke of a pen. Is this a virtuous reason to enter the law? Not at all. Prestige is the other side of this coin. Once we have an "Esq" after our names, some of us get a feeling of superiority and feel empowered.

I Want to Help Change the World

This reason has the greater good written all over it. Some go into law hoping to create change, whether through case law, representing the less fortunate, or taking on worthy causes. I admire those who do this. For the brave souls who choose this path, the issues hit them like a brick in the head when the student loan bills start to roll in. Some find it difficult to stay on this lower-paid path very long, unless they have family money or spousal support. The Internet is littered with stories of those with this calling who end up in poverty and on food stamps.

However, I believe that anything is possible, and I sincerely hope that more people in the practice of law who create ideas to help others can make a good living at it.

I Like Intellectual Challenge

A select few enter the legal life thinking that the profession can challenge them in ways that other professions cannot. The plain fact is, there is little intellectual challenge in law. Most of what we do as lawyers is very dry, bland, and boring.

I Want to Be a Glamorous Litigator

Sorry to be the bearer of bad news, but as someone in the litigation game myself, I can tell you that there is absolutely no glamour or charm in being a lawsuit antagonist or protagonist! The stress and long hours of litigation practice take their toll. The court dramas you see on television and in the movies just are not found in the real world. The lawyers who actually do get cases like those portrayed are one in a million.

I Don't Have a Reason

Due to the "recession," many college graduates end up in law school simply because their degree fields don't offer any job prospects. In other words, they don't have any real reason to be in law school. The people in this group are the most troubling. Law school is an expensive choice and is not a solution to an inability to find meaningful, relevant employment. *The law is **not** the right career choice for most people.*

The Low-Down Reality on the Big Bucks

A select few top-tier law school graduates today may find high-paying jobs, but at what price? Extremely long hours, severe pressure to bill for more time than is humanly possible, and no life balance is the reality. Does this sound like something you want?

The law is not the only profession that has become focused on money. Medicine used to be all about patient welfare and preventing disease, but most doctors today are in it for the money. In days of old, doctors would spend time with patients and counsel them on health and prevention. Unfortunately, doctors are now influenced by drug companies and aren't looking for the newest ways to improve health. Most are pill pushers. Once doctors become licensed, the drug companies are their main source of any new information on the craft!

When I graduated from college in 1993, I had a choice of paths: get an MBA and a management position, or sell high-end real estate. Overwhelmingly, though, the law called out to me, so I answered it! After fifteen years in the law, I have tapped into my true life's purpose, beginning with this book. My years of feeling at war with other attorneys opened me up to wanting to make a difference in the only profession I've really ever known. There is no standing on the sidelines for me anymore. I intend to make the world a much better place than it was when I entered it, and I'll start with our profession!

Law School

Let's get real. Law schools are a business for making money, as are all schools, public or private. The following quote applies to law school as well as business school:

> Business schools make a fortune forcing their students to take in a HUGE amount of information. The majority of it is theoretical. The majority of that is useless.
>
> —Josh Kaufman

Let's take a closer look at law student numbers. American Bar Association (ABA) statistics give us a pretty clear idea of where we are. These stats took my breath away when I saw them:

	2011–12	1963–64
Number of law schools	201	135
Enrolled students	156,458	49,552
Degrees awarded	44,495	9,638
USA population[††]	311,705,000	189,242,000

[††]http://www.americanbar.org/content/dam/aba/administrative/
legal_education_and_admissions_to_the_bar/statistics/
enrollment_degrees_awarded.authcheckdam.pdf

The developments are unreal. The number of graduates and students has more than quadrupled since the sixties, while the population as a whole has yet to even double. There are just too many of us! It is the major reason for our slide downward. I've noted that the dramatization of the law in our popular culture has contributed to the unprecedented demand, and the standard parental guidance, "become a doctor or a lawyer," continues. Increased demand for seats in law school has caused an increase in the number of schools. How many are enough? How many lawyers are enough?

More new lawyers flowing into the system at the current rates will do nothing but make things worse—much worse. If you think it is bad now, you have seen nothing yet. Why have the powers that be allowed such expansion to spiral out of control? It is our job to help spread the word about this problem. Everyone I hear of that wants to attend law school gets a good dose of reality from me, and if you choose to, do the same. We need to shift the perception that has been created over the years.

A *Really* Tough Job Market

You graduate after four years of college, it takes you three years to get your juris doctor, and you pass the bar. There must be jobs out there, right? Lo and behold, there are none, and no prospects either. Then you get the notice from your student loan holder that your payments will begin shortly. And you have on average $125,000 or more to pay back! This is a scary proposition, but one that needn't continue.

Law students (and those considering it) should understand that law school is just a business. If you are going to invest upward of $150,000 (not to mention the additional cost in interest over a thirty-year amortization), you should do some due diligence. If you fail to heed its warnings, then take responsibility for your inability to find a job.

I know this is harsh, but do an Internet search on "attending law school" and see what comes up. It is amazing how many anti-law-school websites are out there. I searched on this exact query and found that the top hit is a Forbes.com article entitled, "Why Attending Law School is the Worst Career Decision You'll Ever Make."[‡‡] It quotes the *Wall Street Journal* announcing that only 55 percent of graduates from the class of 2011 were gainfully employed! The American Bar Association furnished this data. Still want to go to law school? Or stay there? The article also stated: "The message that law school is no longer a sure bet when it comes to employment security and financial prosperity finally seems to be sinking in for potential students." On a positive note, the writer stated that applications are down by about 25 percent, which is good news. It is time for law schools all over the country to revisit their business plans, make the decision to become pickier, and tighten their requirements.

For a really blunt take on why law school is not a good idea, see "Why You Should *Not* Go to Law School."[§§] Aside from the laughs, its points hit the nail on the head: most people don't belong in law school.

An article in *Men's Health* magazine entitled "Is Grad School for Dummies?" took a look at the idea of going back to school as "a way to ride out a bad economy." They said that universities are awarding twice as many graduate degrees as they were twenty years ago and that student loan debt for these degrees is $1 trillion. The article

---

[‡‡] http://www.forbes.com/sites/jmaureenhenderson/2012/06/26/why-attending-law-school-is-the-worst-career-decision-youll-ever-make/

[§§] http://www.huffingtonpost.com/tucker-max/law-school_b_2713943.html

likened the degrees to "any investment" you can make, such as in a stock or bond. It also delved into the pros and cons of MBAs, law degrees, and PhDs. As to the law degree, it said if you are a top-tier undergrad *and* attend a top-tier law school, then do it. If not, then be very wary of the debt and the lack of jobs you'll face.

The idea of "inherent value" in higher education is not a given any longer. Even master's degrees do not provide the benefit they once did. An article on CNNMoney.com entitled "My Master's Wasn't Worth It"*** is one of a slew you can find on the Internet. In my estimation, finding your life's purpose and moving in its direction may be well more important than any degree. Postponing your ideals to go to school may not work to your advantage. If you or someone you know is considering law school, it is best to weigh all your options *very* carefully.

Underemployment and the Issues with "Hanging a Shingle"

Currently, newly licensed lawyers are also plagued with another big issue: many are "employed," yet the word doesn't mean much. Many cannot find full-time jobs, so they accept contract work, small projects, court appearances, and the like. So what do lawyers who find themselves in this predicament do? More and more of them are starting their own law firms, which means they are jumping into the practice without any real-world experience. Anyone who has been to one can testify to the fact that a law school can't teach that. It takes years of working as an associate with a mentor or boss to amass enough experience to properly and successfully represent clients.

Another interesting article on the unemployment challenge for graduates is *Business Insider*'s "10 Faces Behind the Incredible Law

---

***http://money.cnn.com/gallery/news/economy/2013/01/24/masters-degree-debt/index.html

School Underemployment Crisis."[†††] It highlights ten licensees who were unable to find gainful employment; some were unable to pay their bills and needed food stamps, while others went to live with their parents. The stories are telling of our current reality.

There are some real ramifications and consequences of all of this. What does it mean for other attorneys and the clients of these novices? First, their clients have more than likely hired incompetent counsel, though passing the bar supposedly creates competency. Some might argue that new lawyers can research the law and learn as they go, but that does not take into account the nuances of the business of law or the way the real world works.

Additionally, most of these newcomers don't really know what they're doing and seem to think their lack of knowledge can be overcome by the use of threats, intimidation, bullying, and yelling at opposing counsel. They believe that the louder they are, the better their point is made. Chapter 16 discusses the huge need for mentoring these attorneys so they can develop into respected members of their profession and communities.

Legal Education

The way we educate law students follows the same tradition it has for well over a hundred years. The time has come to overhaul the way we educate our law students. Up through the present, we've taught them:

- The Socratic method
- Common law
- Case law
- Ethics rules

[†††] http://www.businessinsider.com/real-stories-behind-the-law-school-crisis-2012-4?op=1

What we should teach our students:

- Real-world problem solving
- The current state of different areas of the law
- How to best counsel clients
- Business training and all aspects of running a law firm
- Integrity in decision making

Gone are the days when the Socratic method was useful, if it ever was. The method does not teach us how to think like real-world lawyers. There are some thoughtful arguments for doing away with it and for keeping it, as those that law professors give in the December 2011 *New York Times* article, "Rethinking How the Law Is Taught."‡‡‡ I believe there is always a better way, and the time has come for Socrates to be replaced with teaching students how to practice law.

If we look at each and every core class in law school, we find that none teach how to operate in the real world. Outdated and stale general principles are the current standard. Yes, these classes are intended to give an overview of the law, but we need to integrate the nitty-gritty of the day-to-day into them. It is time to create curricula that teach *how* to practice law and run a law firm. Law schools and their governance have been unwilling to change with the times, and it shows. Are you involved in the legal education system, or could you have a positive influence on the process? If so, what can you do to make things better?

---

‡‡‡ http://www.nytimes.com/roomfordebate/2011/12/15/rethinking-how-the-law-is-taught

The Bar Exam and the System

Once I began practicing law in a way that was meaningful to me, I started to ponder what the LSAT, law school, and the bar had to do with real life. I looked back on what it had taken me to become a practicing attorney and wondered what it had to do with what lawyers actually did day to day.

The LSAT is supposed to evaluate potential success in law school, and so we assume that it is effective at testing our reasoning skills. Then we assume that law school will prepare us for the world of lawyering. The bar exam is then supposed to validate our competency to operate out in the world. How does it provide an adequate barrier against those who aren't ready to be lawyers? The answer is that it doesn't. Then most of us have to take a test on ethics and personal responsibility, which, if we pass, allows for licensure. Last but not least, in many jurisdictions, we are required to take a multiday class on "professionalism" within a certain time after being licensed.

The education and bar examination systems need a complete overhaul and reconstruction. Until that happens, we should set up a mentoring system to help guide newly inducted attorneys.

Making a Difference

What ideas do you have for making our legal education system better? You have the power to create change! How can you make a difference? Call, write, or e-mail your law school and the ABA. Reach out to others who can help you implement your ideas.

If you are considering law school or know someone who is, please see the Resources Section at the end of the book.

PART TWO

Then and Now

PART TWO

The first thing we do, let's kill all the lawyers.
—Shakespeare, *Henry VI,* Part 2

It is difficult to fix the time when the profession took a wrong turn or declare why it did so. The reasons will be subject to debate for a long time.
—Carl T. Bogus, "The Death of an Honorable Profession," *Indiana Law Journal*

Where Did We Take the Wrong Turn?

As I accumulated research and interviewed attorneys who had practiced in the sixties, I found that the law used to be quite different from the way it is today. For thousands of years, all business was done with mutual promises and a handshake. No long-winded, multipage contracts. Both parties' words were their bond. Their reputations and livelihoods rested on the promise of what the parties agreed to. When a dispute or disagreement arose, most of the time, lawyers never even got involved. But when they did, problems were solved quickly and easily, without the protracted litigation so often seen in the past three decades.

What happened to our profession? As Mr. Bogus stated, many might think that it is difficult to discern. After many years of research, here is what I've found.

About the effects of supply and demand: the 1970s saw a sharp increase in attorneys joining the profession, and it's been worse since. The increases created a simple supply-and-demand problem: too many attorneys and not enough legitimate business to go around. Among other things, this led to the rise of negligence law.

Our society created what I like to call the "blame game" in the 1970s. Attorneys looking for a way to make a living in an already fully packed legal profession were drawn to personal injury law, which became a niche and has grown exponentially since. This niche has morphed into the mass-marketed mess that we have today, with attorneys who use "used-car salesman" tactics in their advertising and marketing. The strategy includes the use of billboards, TV commercials, radio ads, and the Internet to drive would-be clients who have been somehow "wronged" to the lawyer for "help."

Public perception of the profession has been severely impacted by this type of marketing and the actions of these clients and their attorneys. I cringe every time I see one of those ads. Why did the profession ever allow this kind of marketing? More important, why do *we* continue to allow it?

Manufacturing Lawsuits and the Dirty Secrets of Litigation

The practice of law is a service-based business, but a large number of attorneys have taken to manufacturing conflict. These crafty folks prove that the profession does not suffer from a lack of intellect—just a lack of integrity. Instead of looking for inspiration in some area of the law that is productive and beneficial to others, they've chosen to create disputes based on loopholes (areas where statutes are not specific) or on the good chance that a defendant will settle when faced with potential costs. This lawsuit mentality has created a society that is afraid of stepping out to do anything meaningful or outside the box for fear of getting sued for some reason or another. Society has become so litigious that it has stifled a lot of the entrepreneurial spirit— which was once part of what made this country an amazing place to live and do business.

In *The Collapse of the Common Good*, Philip Howard discusses how our country has become paralyzed by lawyers and the fear arising from the lawsuit culture our profession ushered in. Litigiousness has made our everyday lives a whole lot more expensive over the last thirty years. Insurance of any kind is more expensive than it used to be, as is the cost of anything you buy, due to past or possible future costs of litigation. The cost of a company either suing or being sued is now built into everything we buy. I know that some will argue that the culprit of spiraling prices is inflation, which is true, but we have to take into account our profession's impact on society as a whole.

About thirty or so years ago, legal practice started moving away from general to specialty based. Nowadays, even in small towns, the general practitioner is nowhere to be found. Why did this happen? We can surmise. Our federal, state, and local governments have created so many new laws over the years (mostly to try to control citizens), that the need for specialized practitioners grew. Back in the day, many lawyers were able to handle most kinds of law needed in daily life, from divorces and home purchases to business contracts. It was much easier to be in general practice then, since there was less regulation: simply, fewer laws.

Of the most adversarial areas of law, family law, tort law, and employment law seem to be at the top of the list, though civil litigation and criminal law are always on it. Attorneys in these kinds of law know that most lawsuits in them have payouts if they play the system correctly. The "nuisance" lawsuit is therefore very common. It's like these lawyers are using legal loopholes and fear as loaded guns to "hold up" others, literally and figuratively *stealing* from them. "Give me all your money!" Yet, these claims and suits are not based on much but loose conjecture.

Adding insult to injury, most judges are not willing to toss these cases where they belong: in the garbage. Many of our state judges are elected, and as such, they are more concerned with keeping a low profile in the courtroom. They refuse to enter summary judgment, thereby forcing the parties to mediate. They won't make a decision, yet are also afraid of one being overturned on appeal. So, many judges put off making any major rulings in hope that the parties will settle and that the cases will just go away. Not to say that there are not decent and honest judges out there—the ones who will make the right decisions. I implore judges everywhere: please look at how you operate your courtroom. Please lose the fear of elections and do the right thing! We are all part of the solution.

Litigators have other tricks in their arsenals. Clearly, there are always at least two sides to every disagreement. In most disputes, whether personal or business, each side thinks it is right and the other wrong. Any smart litigator always discloses to clients the possibility of losing at trial. However, if these attorneys were truthful and honest about the *real* economic costs and aggravation of litigation, most lawsuits would never even get filed. But the lawyer sees big dollar signs and billable hours. Another point is that once suit is filed and the parties served, there is usually no turning back. With litigation in full effect, the egos of all parties get tightly engaged, starting an extremely nonproductive and wasteful process.

The attorneys get well paid, and in the end the clients or judge "split the baby" (the claim gets sliced down the middle). But a large percentage of cases are settled before they get to trial, since trials are quite a gamble. All litigators know this intimately! So why not split everything from the get-go and save everyone hassle and money? And we wonder why we are the butt of so many jokes.

In yesteryear, counsel would pick up the phone and call the other side and work it out right there. No threats, yelling, or filings at the courthouse. We can be part of reviving this way of practicing once again, and it all comes down to honesty. Be totally (and when you have to, brutally) honest with your client, the other side, and *yourself*. When your goal is to help your clients, abundance abounds if you believe in and create it (as we will discuss in Chapter 13). Word gets around quickly when you are doing the right thing—and when you're not! If you cannot make a living by doing the right thing and with positive client word of mouth, then you need to find another profession. It is that easy. We need to put an end to all attorney advertising and do business the way it has always been done, which is with word of mouth and building a sphere of influence through trust and honor.

Winning—No Matter What

Does it make sense to do whatever it takes to win a case? Understandably, clients want to win, so they end up putting massive pressure on their attorneys to make it happen. Such clients should be dismissed from your office, and they need to be called out on their actions. If your client has no integrity, how can you? The law *does* allow for nondisclosure of facts in litigation. If the other side doesn't ask, then don't tell. What if both sides were honest, truthful, and forthcoming with the good and the bad in their respective cases?

Disputes would not turn into litigation. Everyone would benefit, and the lawyers would make less money.

Does making less money on a lawsuit make you cringe? Your beliefs about money create your income. We need a paradigm shift in this regard. You most definitely create ideal income by attracting your ideal clients and making all your decisions with integrity. Some of you won't or can't believe this is possible, but I have done it for the past fifteen years. You just need to know how, and you can learn the basic framework (which we'll begin exploring in Chapter 8).

Remember WhoCanISue.com and SueEasy.com? It can be hard to believe that this kind of stuff is out there. I understand that there is some limited need for those who have been injured to be able to right a wrong, but things are out of control! Since legislatures are controlled by fellow attorneys, tort reform is not on the table right now. But as you will soon learn, we don't need any new laws to create change in the profession.

The Dirty Three

I may not make many friends of those who practice in these areas, but I have to speak my mind. A quick caveat, this section is not meant to be a blanket statement about *all* lawyers who call these three niches their practice areas, as I know plenty of really honest lawyers who call these areas their main practice in the law. The following types of law all have a place, and things must change in so many areas of the law, not just these. However, these three niches have done the most damage to the public image of our profession and have wreaked economic havoc as well.

1. Criminal Lawyers. There are some really decent and honest criminal lawyers out there. I know a few. Criminal law attorneys feel their job, in most cases, is to make sure the prosecutors do *their* jobs, regardless of whether their clients are truly guilty or not. Understanding that those charged with crimes will say they didn't do it no matter what, many did, so they should do the time. The system is broken in any case, but that doesn't mean that the prosecutors and defense lawyers cannot both have integrity in the process.

2. Mass Tort and Class Action Lawyers. This kind of lawsuit has been abused for a very long time, and it is time to really limit it and make it about the client, not the attorneys. The lawyers make all the money, and the plaintiffs get squat. It's understandable that anytime you hear someone who is not a lawyer speak of class action suits, they do it with disgust in their voices.

3. Personal Injury Lawyers. This kind of law most embodies all that is wrong in our profession. Granted, some clients need this area of the law, but I believe there are very few. That's why the commercials and billboards are there, and they attract the kind of client who wants to take advantage of the system and make money off some "injury." The attorneys who accept these clients know the system and play it well, to society's detriment.

On an almost daily basis you can find a story of some almost unimaginable new lawsuit. A woman was accidentally hit by a Little League baseball at a game. She had been standing close to where a pitcher—a little kid—was warming up. So she decided to sue his parents. The utter disregard for honesty in these kinds of lawsuits is appalling. How long will we stand for this?

Advertising

Nowadays, you see lawyers everywhere: billboards, television (especially during the day), the Internet, and of course, print media. Let's be brutal here: how the hell have we allowed attorneys to advertise like this? What happened to the way things were always done, such as getting known by word of mouth, building a sphere of influence, and being referred by those who know your work and trust you? The new kinds of advertising cheapen our profession and make us look like used-car salesmen. No offense to those who sell pre-owned cars!

Dramatization of Law in the Media

The chart below clearly indicates of how the media, beginning the 1950s, began dramatizing the legal profession. From what I can tell, the book *To Kill a Mockingbird*, and its subsequent movie, were the beginning of this movement. Decade by decade, you see the amount of media increasing, and this isn't the whole story. During the 1990s, there was a huge spike, and for the next twenty years it continued with television shows, books, and movies that make the profession out to be something it is not.

I was a college student in the 1990s and was impacted by all of this drama. It surely influenced my decision to join the profession.

A Brief History of Media Dramatization

BOOKS

1950 - 59	1960 - 69	1970 - 79	1980 - 89	1990 - 99	2000 - 09	2010 - 13
The Drowning Pool - 50	To Kill a Mockingbird - 60	The Guilty Thing Surprised - 70	Rage of Angels - 80	The Firm - 92	The Appeal - 08	
The Judge & his Hangman - 54	The Chinese Nail Murders - 61	Murder at the Savoy - 70	Paris Trout - 89	The Client - 99	The Brethren - 00	
A Murder is Announced - 50	The Final Deduction - 61	The Chain of Chance - 75		The Partner - 98	The Lincoln Lawyer - 05	
Vengeance is Mine! - 50		Death of an Expert Witness - 77		The Chamber - 95	The King of Torts - 03	
Gideon's Day - 55		A Judgement in Stone - 77		Suspicion of Guilt - 96	The Color of Law - 05	
Scales of Justice - 55				The Street Lawyer - 98	Devil's Corner - 08	
The Law - 57					Open and Shut - 03	

TELEVISION SHOWS

1950 - 59	1960 - 69	1970 - 79	1980 - 89	1990 - 99	2000 - 09	2010 - 13
Not for Hire - 59	The Defenders - 61	The D.A. - 71	L.A. Law - 86	Ally McBeal - 97	100 Centre St - 01	Blue Bloods - 10
Perry Mason - 57	The Lawyer - 69	Owen Marshall - 71	Matlock - 86	Family Law - 99	Boston Legal - 04	The Defenders - 10
		Petrocelli - 74	The People's Court	JAG - 95	Close to Home - 05	Fairly Legal - 11
		Young Lawyers - 70		Judge Judy - 96	Conviction - 06	Franklin & Bash - 11
				Judging Amy - 99	The Court - 02	Harry's Law - 11
				Law & Order - 90	The Good Wife - 09	
				Law & Order SVU - 99	Just Legal - 05	
				Michael Hayes - 97	Justice - 06	
				Murder One - 95	Kevin Hill - 04	
				The Practice - 97	Law & Order - Criminal Intent - 01	

MOVIES

1950 - 59	1960 - 69	1970 - 79	1980 - 89	1990 - 99	2000 - 09	2010 - 13
Witness for the Prosecution - 57	To Kill a Mockingbird - 62	The Paper Chase - 73	The Verdict - 82	Presumed Innocent - 90	Erin Brockovich - 00	The Lincoln Lawyer - 11
12 Angry Men - 57		And Justice For All - 79	The Accused - 88	My Cousin Vinny - 92	Find Me Guilty - 06	Conviction - 10
Anatomy of a Murder - 59			Breaker Morant - 80	A Few Good Men - 92	Beyond a Reasonable Doubt - 00	The Conspirator - 10
			Body Heat - 81	A Civil Action - 98	Intolerable Cruelty - 03	Conviction - 10
			Irreconcilable Differences - 84	A Time to Kill - 96	Rules of Engagement - 00	
			Music Box - 89		North County - 05	
			Gideon's Trumpet - 80		Legally Blonde - 01	

This chart can also be viewed at: www.RaisingtheBarBook.com/mediadrama.

The first John Grisham book I ever read, *The Firm*, was a revelation to me. It was one of the first books I could not put down until I finished it. He is a master craftsman, weaving together his plots and subplots, keeping his readers on the edges of their seats. Grisham's topics in his many novels encompass all the reasons that people choose the law—money, prestige, helping the less fortunate, fighting for a worthwhile cause, and the like. Over the years, this large-scale dramatization of the profession has been done in every way possible, and it may largely account for why so many of us have flocked to the law. I was an avid reader of Scott Turow along with Grisham, and ate up television shows like *LA Law* and, more recently, *Boston Legal*.

How many TV shows, movies, books, and the like are out there about lawyers? Practicing attorneys know that our day-to-day lives are nowhere near as dramatic in comparison to these fabricated ones. The law isn't exciting, fun-filled, or full of money and fame. For the most part, it is boring, repetitive, and full of stress.

What's the correlation between the upward trend in the number of attorneys and the increase in the dramatization of the law? I believe that the fictions are a big part of the problem. Further, it hasn't helped that we have a nation of parents that routinely suggest that children become lawyers or doctors; I heard mine say it often. They wrongly assumed that the law was a great way to earn a living, and parents continue to preach the same message, even today. Our parents have clearly been influenced by the barrage of content over the years.

A Time of Honor and Respect
CHAPTER 5

> Lawyers have made exceptional contributions throughout the history of the Republic. They have been able to do so, in large part, because of the powers of critical thinking and practical judgment; but equally important has been the fact that lawyers have considered themselves part of a profession entrusted with special responsibilities. They were inspired to be not merely technicians, but statesmen.
>
> —Carl T. Bogus, *Indiana Law Journal*

In the 1960s and before, law was dramatically different from today. Attorneys were revered and respected, and most were ethical and honest. Business was done with verbal agreements and a handshake. A promise was a sacred bond and trust with another person. Contracts were in most instances one page long.

Many would say that the reason behind lengthy contracts, people's failure to abide by their promises, and our litigiousness can be solely blamed on our profession. But as lawyers only helped and supported people who didn't live up to their end of the bargain, this isn't the main reason for the downfall. Society's integrity in general has also taken a downward trajectory. Agreements aren't honored and promises end up broken. The masses know that they can always find an attorney to help find a "loophole" to get them out of the responsibility of their agreements.

Life was a whole lot simpler for attorneys who practiced in the 1960s and before. A whole lot fewer lawyers meant the cutthroat world we live in today just didn't exist, and neither did the extreme stress that many of us encounter every day in the profession. Life was more laid-back, and technology didn't have us feeling "on call" twenty-four hours a day, seven days a week. Referrals were made by word of mouth or on one's reputation in the community, and it was easier to make a comfortable living.

The United States was founded by lawyers. Twenty-five of the fifty-six[§§§] signers of the Declaration of Independence were attorneys! For most of United States history, attorneys were respected, honored, and important members of society. As we know, this is not the case anymore. We are no longer a profession; the practice of law has become a business. There is no honor in it for most anymore; it is all about the money. The attorney members of the Founding Fathers would be sad and ashamed of what we have become.

So what was law like before the seventies? From my interviews, I learned that almost nothing was done for hourly fees; most work was flat-fee based. Word got around quickly if someone didn't act honestly and in the clients' best interests. None of the shenanigans that happen today would ever have been put up with. You would have been quickly out of business! Isn't it time that we make our way back to simple once again?

[§§§] http://www.nps.gov/foju/upload/take2.pdf

PART THREE

The Awakening

10 Steps to Awakening

10	**The Ideal Life**
9	**Emotions**
8	**Balance**
7	**Intention**
6	**Meditation**
5	**Present Moment**
4	**Beliefs**
3	**Intuition**
2	**Integrity**
1	**Life Purpose**

The Alarm Sounds
CHAPTER 6

If humanity does not opt for integrity we are through completely. It is absolutely touch and go. Each one of us could make the difference.

—Richard Buckminster Fuller

Don't Hit the Snooze Button!

Chances are, you have been asleep for most of your life, lulled there by the thoughts and beliefs of others. It is time to wake up and take back control of your life and your destiny. I present below my Ten Steps, which could possibly transform your career and your life. That's all up to you and your willingness to consider what is and what could be. This book is here to support you, whether you think your life passions lie somewhere outside the law or want to reconnect with the reasons you decided to be in it. From here, it's all about infinite possibilities for your life and waking up to your ideals. When we start living every day from this awakened state, we change inside, and that has an effect on the outside world and the profession.

I have spent the last twenty-five years of my life learning, exploring, compiling, and then distilling down what I am about to share with you. It has transformed the core of my being, and if you open up to it, you may find the same is true for you. Some of the ideas you may never have heard or been exposed to before. You'll learn of some best practices for life and business as well as universal principles that much of the ancient world knew. It is time for us all to reconnect deeply to it all.

Most human beings are asleep. They operate their daily lives from a place of powerlessness. They allow marketers, their families, and the media to influence their every decision. We are like caged animals, penned up and controlled. There are so many influencers out there; everywhere you look, your attention is being vied for. Websites, television, magazines, social media, marketers, governments, religions, and the like all vie for your money and send you messages based on fear. Fear is the most powerful motivator used on this planet, and it has been since our species began. The herd lives life on autopilot, effectively asleep to the mind control—and therefore to the unlimited possibilities that exist in their lives.

Over the years, you have been told what to think, what to eat, how to act, and what life should be like. It is time to start taking responsibility for each and every one of your thoughts. It is time to figure out what you want and choose to believe, and to create your life the way you design it. Knowledge is power, and the more you understand about the way the universe operates, the more powerful you become.

"Out There"

Most of humanity thinks that for things to change, we need to focus on taking action in the outside world, but instead, I have found that change starts in you and me. Awakening (and each of the Ten Steps) is about how we can change to align with what we would like to see both personally and in the world. There will always be those in any profession whose basis for life is greed, but we surely don't need to seek out and try to change those we think are not on the right path. Further, we don't need to make more laws or rules to stop behaviors we don't like, since someone who is inclined to break a rule or law will do it regardless (or find a way around it through a loophole). The Internet will eventually expose those who are not honorable. Clients will begin to expect honor and integrity from our profession when we begin to expect it from them.

> Faith is taking the first step even when you don't see the whole staircase.
>
> —Martin Luther King Jr.

Be Open to a New Self

To get the most out of this book, please have a *completely* open mind. Approach what you read as pointing the way to infinite possibilities for supporting you in moving forward and toward personal growth. It applies whether you choose to stay in the law or follow your heart into something different.

Exploration:
- What are the reasons you chose the law?
- Why did you go to law school?
- What were your intentions when you first started practicing?
- What have you created in your career in the law to date?
- Has your experience been ideal?
- What have you enjoyed? Not enjoyed?
- What are your ideals, goals, and intentions for your future in the law?
- What do you believe about the following:
  - Other lawyers and the profession?
  - Making money? Success?

- Operating from a place of honor in your business and personal life?
- Your clients?
- Your area(s) of practice?

I'm trying to free your mind, Neo, but I can only show you the door. You're the one that has to walk through it.

—Morpheus, *The Matrix*

What would it be like to *free* your mind? I open the door for those who are ready.

Integrity

| 1 | Life Purpose |

Step #1 Your Life Purpose
CHAPTER 7

When you follow your bliss…
doors will open where you would not have
thought there would be doors; and where there
wouldn't be a door for anyone else.

—Joseph Campbell

If there are more than 1.25 million licensed attorneys in our country and we cannot support this number financially, then there must be *hundreds of thousands* who would be much happier in some other profession. The lure and magnetism of the law has been hard to resist, but the time has come for a mass exodus. However, those who want to stay have many options to ensure that they have a positive impact on society and their clients.

Success is waking up in the morning, whoever you are, wherever you are, however old or young, and bounding out of bed because there's something out there you love to do, that you believe in, that you're good at—something that's bigger than you are, and you can hardly wait to get at it again today.

—Whit Hobbs

Transitioning out of the law (or any career, for that matter) can be one of the most difficult life decisions. There are even consultants nowadays who specialize in helping lawyers in their transitions out.

This was unheard of in the past. Not everyone needs a coach or consultant to accomplish this, and there are many books that discuss the topic in depth.

I assume that tens of thousands of us do want to transition out. I can understand the fear of the process. We spend many years and boatloads of money to become attorneys, so the "sunk cost fallacy" can keep us where we are, for one thing. But if you take the time to plan, discuss, and delve into what you really want to do with your life, transitioning can become easy. I have been through the very same fears, thoughts, and decisions, and will share with you my own transition process. Once you decide to follow your heart, your life will never be the same!

> There are two great days in our lives: The day we are born and the day we discover why.
>
> —John C. Maxwell

How Do You Find Your Life Purpose?

Is your heart forever and indelibly in love with the practice of law? If not, then what might your unique contribution to this world look like? What if you are OK with being a lawyer but are just not sure if the profession is your purpose? Would you be much happier doing something different? If you can't answer these kinds of questions right now, don't worry. Answers will come when you open up to them. The first step is just to ask.

Once I decided to delve into the possibility of leaving the law, I sought out books, documentaries, and other information on how others were able to find their callings. What I found was that life is very different for those who have connected with their purposes. These folks jump out of bed and cannot wait to get into their days, knowing they are making a difference doing something they love.

I believe we all have a higher purpose or a calling, and when we heed the call, our inner worlds open—and so does the outer world. Our hearts send us messages, usually faint at first, but ever increasing in volume until they are hard for us to ignore. We can listen to the signals and start to move in that expanded direction or ignore them altogether; we all have free will. When we ignore these yearnings (and many of us do), life can be awful and difficult at best. Are you at the point where you want to scream, "This sucks!"? I have met so many of us who are—as was I.

Why do we ignore these signs if our lives could move instead in such an amazing direction? The answer is fear. It stops us in our tracks. Fear of the unknown, coupled with the feeling of certainty we have of the known. Then add in the issues with leaving all the schooling, work, experience, and money we've laid on the table as lawyers. For some, it is easier to stay put, even though their lives are miserable.

"Feel the fear and do it anyway" has been a mainstream concept for some time (and is the title of a book). So why let fear stop you from pursuing something you would absolutely love? As I will show, we really only experience two emotions: fear and love. Any other emotion is just an offshoot or variation of one of them. And it can be simple to let go of fear in any of its iterations. As the saying goes, the key is to just *feel* it and move forward. We have been taught from early in our lives that it is not good to feel anything we judge as "bad." Is your life worth moving toward the joy of a career you would love, or would you rather just stay stuck and miserable?

> The way you get meaning into your life is to devote yourself to loving others, devote yourself to your community around you, and devote yourself to creating something that gives you purpose and meaning.
>
> —Mitch Albom

I knew the law was not my true calling early on, but I wouldn't admit it to myself for many years. I experienced the same fears as anyone who knows he or she is destined for something other than the law. I wondered how I could give up all the work of the past twenty years, and all the money, time, and sweat I had invested in my career as a lawyer. I decided to let go of the fear and move in the direction of my life's purpose every day. This all led me to the desire to write this book and share my journey with others.

Just below, I have provided you with a condensed framework to get you *moving* in the direction of your purpose.

Life Purpose Framework

Consider the following questions (and journal the answers if you feel it would be beneficial).

What do you:
- Love to do?
- Love to learn about?
- Read about most often?
- Excel at?
- Get excited or passionate about?
- Talk to others about?
- Consider your greatest strengths and weaknesses?
- Think you would do with your time if money was no issue?

Is there a common theme in your answers? If so, you may be getting closer to (or have found) what you really love. If not, just ask the questions and the universe will bring you the answers when the time is right. You just need to open up and be present enough to hear your intuition and then listen to it. When I asked myself these questions, the answers started to make themselves known, and with some contemplation and meditation, it became crystal clear to me what I was here to do.

We each have many gifts that make us unique. The problem I see is that many of us hide these gifts from the world. Isn't it time to share your gifts with the world? Do you love animals, photography, business, teaching, or art? Would you really love to write a book or share your expertise on a topic?

Once you figure out what makes you connect with the passion and love that is available in your purpose, the people, places, and things you will need start to appear. As Joseph Campbell said in the quote at the beginning of this chapter, "doors will open where you would not have thought there would be doors."

I have had the opportunity to use this framework as a point of discussion with some of my lawyer friends and acquaintances. As I walked them through the ideas—about what they love, what they have passion for, and the like, some came upon possibilities quickly. For others, it took some time. What I really loved was seeing their eyes light up after the thoughts "Wow, I could really do this for a living!" and "How great would my life be!" Many of them had questions for me about how they could monetize their passions. The answer I normally give here is that people need to allow their hearts and intuition to find ways to make their passions a reality. I go further into the topic in Chapter 9.

The Internet is a powerful tool for researching your ideas, and also offers amazing opportunities to make money with them. Since most of us have been locked away in our offices practicing law, we have failed to notice the multitude of ways to use the Internet to sell products and information. The very idea that you can sell someone else's products to make money astounds everyone I speak with.

There's a great audio program published by Nightingale-Conant, I found a couple of years ago called *More Money, More Life*, by Stephen Pierce. The program can open you up to a ton of ideas on how you can use the Internet to make money. There is no limit what you can find, do, become, or explore. The only limits we really have are the ones we put on ourselves. That being said, it may take some time for you to find something you can really connect with and love, but fear not, keep taking the next step, and the foothold will appear.

My Main Life Purpose

I awaken lawyers by speaking, teaching, writing, and sharing all that I have learned so that they may create their ideal lives, and we can all have a massive impact on the profession and the world.

Being of Service to the World

> The purpose of life is to contribute in some way to making things better.
>
> —Robert F. Kennedy

This world desperately needs people to align with their purposes. There are millions of people, in all kinds of professions, who are not happy with the career they have chosen and don't see any way out or feel there are any options. If more of us all over the planet heard the call and heeded it, what would things be like? Millions of us loving life and living our dreams. The world would truly be a different place!

Do you deserve to be happy? Of course you do. We all do! Our society has programmed us to think that life is difficult and is always a struggle. But life opens up when we do. There could be an amazing new life and career waiting for you to allow it in so that it can become your reality.

Work is love made visible.

—Kahlil Gibran, *The Prophet*

If you would like to read more about finding your way on the path to your life's purpose, I suggest a couple of books that were impactful on me. One is *The Purpose of Your Life*, by Carol Adrienne. Its subtitle tells it all: *Finding Your Place in the World Using Synchronicity, Intuition, and Uncommon Sense*. Then there's *The Passion Test*, by Janet Bray Attwood and Chris Attwood. It walks you through the simple test the authors created to open you up to new ideas and the path to your ideal.

Intuition

2 **Integrity**

Life Purpose

Step #2 Integrity and Honesty
CHAPTER 8

To see what is right and not do it is a lack of courage.

—Confucius

What does it mean to have integrity? Most dictionaries say that integrity implies the qualities of honesty and honor. Synonyms for "integrity" include honesty, probity, rectitude, honor, good character, principle(s), ethics, morals, righteousness, morality, virtue, decency, fairness, scrupulousness, sincerity, truthfulness, and trustworthiness.

It also connotes a whole, undivided, undiminished, or perfect condition. When you compromise your honesty and integrity, you become less than "whole." You lose a bit of your "self" every time you make a decision you know is not aligned with your core.

> Being honest may not get you a lot of friends, but it will always get you the right ones.
>
> —John Lennon

A lack of honesty is what got us into our current predicament. Why does the world seem to lack honesty and integrity today? I believe the main reason is fear, which is pervasive in everyday life. Most of what we see and hear on the TV, radio, or the Internet is fear-based. When you turn on any news program, what do we normally see or hear? Murders, robberies, and negative messages.

Very rarely we find an uplifting segment on something that is right with the world, or someone making a positive impact on others. Over the past ten years most of what we have heard is how bad the world economy is, and how many people are being affected by this issue. When we live from fear and not intention, we make decisions that are not rooted in integrity. Decisions made from fear come from a mind-set called "scarcity consciousness," which is fear of the unknown, stemming from the mass belief that there isn't enough of anything to go around. There isn't enough money, business, love, or food. This is a "dog-eat-dog" and "survival-of-the-fittest" way of thinking, and it is purely a function of the head or the ego. Other common societal beliefs based in scarcity consciousness include:

- The recession is the reason that business is bad.
- It is hard to make money.
- I am not worthy of achieving my dreams.
- I could never have X, Y, or Z because_____.
- My boss doesn't pay me enough, so I will take another job to make up for it (or, I won't work very hard).
- I don't deserve it.

> When our actions are based on good intentions our soul has no regrets.
>
> —Anthony Douglas Williams

In the moments leading up to our choices, what is our thinking like? Do we treat others as we would like to be treated? When we live from a place of total integrity, things shift internally, and the external world does too. Honesty and integrity in our businesses and personal lives have a massive impact on consciousness. Be a role model for your children, family, and friends, and create a ripple effect in the world! No one can *ever* take away your integrity; *you* make the choice to give it away. You have a choice in *every* moment to make a better decision than before. The actions that stem from our decisions are all we have. We can live our lives based in honesty and make a great living doing so. It is time for the law profession and society to do the right thing no matter what. This requires living from our intuition and from the heart. As you will find out in the next Step, science has shown that the heart has its own consciousness.

Exploration:
- What was the last decision you made that you found yourself conflicted about?
- What did you feel?
- What emotions came up for you?
- How did you go about making the decision?
- Was it easy, or did you struggle to make it?
- If you had the opportunity to make a different decision, would you? Why?

For as a man think in his heart, so is he.

—Proverbs 23:7

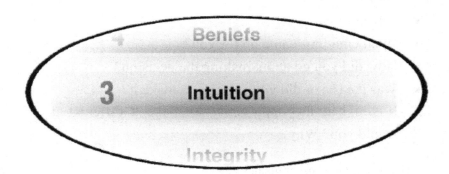

Beniefs

3   Intuition

Integrity

It is the heart always that sees, before the head can see.
—Thomas Carlyle

How can we make decisions firmly based on the principles of integrity, personal responsibility, and honor? The answer is to live from our hearts and intuition. As a society, we have shut off our intuition and refuse to listen to anything but our egos or heads.

Your heart has its own intelligence and energy field. Isn't it peculiar how so many sayings involve the heart? We often hear things like, "You broke my heart," "I love you with all my heart," or that we should "speak from the heart."

We know the truth not only by reason, but also by the heart.
—Blaise Pascal

For the left brainers, there is real science behind this, and the information is quite enlightening. I strongly encourage you to read Doc Childre and Howard Martin's book, *The HeartMath Solution*. It's based on thirty years of scientific research on the heart's own intelligence and how connecting with your heart can reduce stress, open your intuition, and help you to manage your emotions. It really opened my eyes to how powerful the heart truly is, not only in its ability to pump blood every day, but also to guide us. We have to be open and willing to listen to our heart's wisdom.

> We have grown up in a culture that places a high value on reason and tends to be skeptical of anything as "inconclusive" as intuition.
> —Doc Childre and Howard Martin,
> *HeartMath Solution*

> As you connect to your hearts, you will find great strength in your ability to be genuine and honest.
> —Mary Soliel, *Michael's Clarion Call*

Head or Heart? Logic or Intuition?

Believe it or not, when we make decisions, we actually have a choice whether to live from our heads and ego or our hearts and intuition. Ego-based decisions are usually made from a place of fear. This is how our government is running the country (and has for the past hundred years). Ego-based thinking has led to society's current problems; they are the culmination of *all* of the decisions made by lawyers over the past forty years.

Our intuition resides in our hearts and the area around our hearts, though we may "think" with our minds. Living from your heart can be quite easy; you just have to open to it and listen. "Checking in" with your heart on any decision will give you an almost instantaneous answer in the moment. If you need to justify or rationalize a choice, then it is usually not based on your intuition but on thoughts from your head. The compelling research from HeartMath shows that our hearts have their own consciousness and ability to communicate our intuition to us. Why aren't we listening?

You can use your intuition to make any decision. All you have to do is put your attention in the area near your heart, in the middle of your chest or so, to see what kind of feeling you get. Is it light or dense, good or bad? With some practice, this kind of decision making becomes second nature. When you make a decision, let it go and move on.

Our egos love to second-guess and analyze everything, but it is not necessary when we use intuition. In *The Intuitive Way*, Penney Pierce states: "With intuition, we know what we need to know, right when we need to know it. The universe, it seems, doesn't waste time or energy. Intuition presents information to us when we need it, not a moment too soon or too late." When we are guided by this force within us, our focus becomes the highest and best for all, not just ourselves. We impact everything around us. When we operate from integrity and our intuition, we honor our planet and *all* living things. We have become such a consumer-based society that we continue to poison and pollute our beautiful planet. What will be left for our children or future generations? A polluted mess with little ability to sustain the billions who inhabit it.

The reason you found this book is that your intuition attracted you to the messages and the keys to awakening! Chances are, you would not have read as far as you have without an innate desire to wake up.

The authors of *HeartMath Solution* describe our hearts' guidance like this: "In yogic practice, the physical heart is considered both literally and figuratively the guide or internal 'guru' cultivating awareness of one's own heartbeat." Living from the present moment and listening to our "internal guru" is the crux of listening to your intuition. Let your heart be your guide, and your own intuition will be your guru!

We Are All Connected

The "unified field" is the energy field of our universe, and it connects *all* living things. If you have never heard this idea before, do yourself a favor and educate yourself about the latest information that science (and more particularly, consciousness) is teaching us. A great introduction to all of this is the movie *What the Bleep Do We Know!?* It inspired me to research the topic, and in turn, it led me to other movies, a huge stack of books to read, and quite a few workshops. I have condensed what I have learned for you here. (If you wish to explore further, look into Gregg Braden's *The Divine Matrix: Bridging Time, Space, Miracles, and Belief,* which really helped me to understand the science underlying this area. You may be a skeptic at first, like I was, but as I studied, many of my questions about life and the universe were answered.)

Our universe is made up of two things: energy and information. Quantum physics has shown that we are made up mostly of empty space. If we removed all of the space in matter, our *entire* universe would fit on the end of a pin (or at the largest, a quarter dollar, though some scientists even say it would be smaller). At first glance, the concept is quite shocking, but it is a principle that many ancient cultures knew. Regardless, the nature of the universe is the total opposite of what we have believed it to be.

(For a quick read on collective consciousness and an intro to meditation: "Collective Consciousness and Meditation: Are We All Interconnected by an Underlying Field?")[****]

[****] http://www.huffingtonpost.com/jeanne-ball/collective-consciousness-meditation_b_822288.html

My brain is only a receiver. In the Universe there is a core from which we obtain knowledge, strength, inspiration. I have not penetrated into the secrets of this core, but I know it exists.

—Nikola Tesla

The World is Our Mirror

Everyone and everything is truly a "mirror" of what we resist in ourselves. Let me explain. Since we are all energetically interconnected, anything we view as "out there" is really a part of us. We are all of it: good, bad, and indifferent. You choose in any moment how you act or react to anything, and contrary to what you may now believe, you have the ability to choose how you feel and how you think in every moment. You make a choice in every moment whether to be evil, dark, mean, or hurtful, or to love, cherish, and express gratitude. The opposite of every decision is present when you choose any way of being: this is duality at work in our lives. When you resist anything in anyone else, it is just a part of *you* that you resist. When you realize and fully accept that we are all interconnected, what you resist in others and life begins to fade away. The poem that follows captures the essence of these ideas.

The World Is Your Mirror, by unknown

The world is your mirror.
The good you find in others, is in you too.
The faults you recognize in others, are your faults as well.
After all, to recognize something you must know it.

The possibilities you see in others, are possible for you as well.
The beauty you see around you, is your beauty.
The world around you is a reflection, a mirror showing you the person you are.

To change your world, you must change yourself.
See the best in others, and you will be your best.
Give to others, and you will give to yourself.
Appreciate beauty, and you will be beautiful.
Admire creativity, and you will be creative.

Love and you will be loved.
Seek to understand, and you will be understood.
Listen, and your voice will be heard.
Teach and you will learn.

I have come to deeply integrate the notion that every experience we have is just that: an experience. We tend automatically to judge experiences as negative or positive, but they don't need to be labeled as one or the other. We will continue to be provided experiences that contain life lessons over and over until we learn them. This is why you might attract the same kinds of people or situations in your world over and over until you "get it."

Exploration:
- What lessons are you experiencing or avoiding?
- What do you believe about what we just discussed?
- Ask your head, then your heart. Do you get a different answer?
- When was the last time you got angry at someone?
- When did someone piss you off with how they were acting or what they said?
- How did this make you feel? What kind of emotion did it create in you?

Resisting and Persisting

Have you ever heard the statement, "What you resist persists"? Wherever or whatever we put our attention on grows. The universe does not judge whether your attention is on things you would like to attract or not. Things we desire *and* resist end up being drawn to us like a piece of metal to a magnet. Being aware and *observing* your thoughts will help you attract what you want and let go of what you don't. We all have negative thoughts and feel down sometimes. This is the normal ebb and flow of life. But when we consciously direct our attention, we can release our resistance to anything.

We usually judge anything as one of three different qualities: negative, neutral, or positive. As the Abraham Hicks teachings tell us, the more we can move toward neutral from a negative emotion, the better. We will work with this principle a bit more.

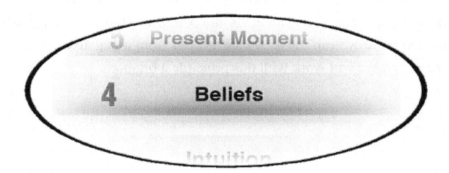

Step #4 You Are Your Beliefs
CHAPTER 10

What is now proved was once imagined.

—William Blake

With every experience, you alone are painting your own canvas, thought by thought, choice by choice.

—Oprah Winfrey

Beliefs Create Our Reality

Whatever you believe causes and creates *everything* in your life. When I say everything, I mean **every single thing, no matter how small or big**. Ponder this for a while and see if you find it to be the case in your own life. You attract or repel based on your beliefs. If you believe is it hard or easy to make money, then it will be. If you think it is easy to gain or lose weight, then it will be. I am sure, being the great lawyers you are, some of you would like to debate this with me. Once you see how the principle has worked in your life, you will soon discover what I did: that your beliefs truly create your everything.

Basically, a belief is just a thought you continue to think, over and over, until it becomes an accepted truth for you. Once an idea is accepted as truth, it embeds itself in the programming of your subconscious mind. This has been proven by quantum physics and shows that whatever the "observer" expects to happen does. Quantum physics is the study of how matter and energy interact. We have learned through science much that the ancient world already knew eons ago. In other words, what the ancients were able to intuit has been proven by quantum physics. When you break the universe down into what it is really made of, science has found that the guts of it are just energy and information. All energy is encoded with information, and matter, as noted earlier, is mostly space, but what is there is made up of energy.

Max Planck, a scientist who worked in the early 1900s, is thought of as the father of this branch of physics. What Planck and many others since have found was that the act of observing matter in their experiments actually had a direct impact on the experiments' end results. The "observer" of the experiment created the result that he or she expected. This is where the idea that we are part of an "observer-created" reality in this universe stemmed from. This idea is thoroughly explained and broken down in *What the Bleep Do We Know!?*

So what does all this have to do with you? Well, you and I are each observers of our individual lives, and as such, whatever we *believe* about anything occurs and is brought into our lives as if we were magnets. Our lives become what we most think about and believe, and all our beliefs are stored in our subconscious. Did you know that not one single scientist has ever been able to show where our thoughts actually come from? Scans of the human brain can show us where a thought registers in it, but not where it comes from. So where do thoughts originate? Something to think about! *What the Bleep* asks, "How far down the rabbit hole do you want to go?"

Before I learned any of these principles, I had limiting beliefs about making money, and so it was a struggle to earn my ideal amount. I believed that it was hard to lose weight, and so it was. I have let go of these limiting thoughts and a whole lot of others, and I reprogrammed myself with new beliefs. If more humans knew how this worked and were able to think for themselves, making changes to their beliefs as they went through life, many more people would be creating their ideal lives. Instead we have the opposite.

For some, the idea behind this Step and the information about quantum physics may be way out there, as they were for me when I first encountered them. Growing up in a rigid, Catholic belief system, we were taught to believe that the opposite was true. I was told, time and time again, that our lives just happen, that we have no control, and that there was some old man in a robe somewhere judging everything I did, said, and thought. Since opening up to the science and my intuition on these topics, I have come to a place where all of them feel right to me. Once I took responsibility for what I wanted to believe about anything and everything, I moved from being miserable in a profession that I wasn't aligned with, seventy-five pounds overweight, in lots of debt, and with little income after the real estate bubble burst. Once I began to shift my beliefs in all these areas (and more), amazing things occurred: I lost thirty pounds in a few months, and have since lost another forty. My income dwarfed most others' in my area of the law and continues to grow. I found my purpose in life and couldn't be happier. So if you doubt that any of this stuff works, read on. We have more to learn about it and how to implement it.

Taking responsibility for our lives demands that we uncover our current beliefs and instill new ones in our mental programming. My career has shifted from practicing law to teaching others how they can and do create "their" reality. This is my purpose. The information I am sharing with you transformed my life.

Taking responsibility for your beliefs and judgments gives you
the power to change them.

—Byron Katie

How do we create our beliefs? First, our parents show us by
example and share with us what they believe about the world, which
of course comes from their parents. This tradition can span many
generations, even thousands of years. In other words, we are
"programmed" by our parents from the time we become able to
communicate. Our families, siblings, friends, radio, television, and
the media all had a hand in how we formed our beliefs, and continue
to daily. It is so important to be conscious of what you hear, see, and
read. When we hear things over and over, the subconscious mind
takes all this in. Anything, no matter how crazy, can become a new
belief. Be vigilantly mindful of the media and how they manipulate
us in everything they do. Some of the advertising out there is pretty
outrageous, especially that of the drug companies. Notice how they
try to talk you into believing you have a condition that requires their
drugs to "cure" it. On television anytime, you can see a drug
company attempting to talk you into depression (or a commercial for
a personal injury attorney)!

I am not saying, though, that we should blame our parents or
families for our beliefs. They did the best they could at their level of
consciousness and with the information they had at the time. For
instance, many in the twentieth century believed that in Christopher
Columbus's day (and medieval times and before), most of the
"civilized" world believed our planet Earth was flat. This has been
shown to be false, and that this was a fallacy that many of us bought
into because we were told this in school.†††† Who really knows what

---

†††† http://en.wikipedia.org/wiki/Myth_of_the_Flat_Earth

is "truth" or not? For all I know this article that I just cited could be wrong! Regardless, there are plenty of examples of how what was once "known" to be the "truth" was disproved. You can proceed with any of your own beliefs: look at each one under a microscope and check into it.

Our beliefs, as I've noted, are not stored in our conscious minds. Most of them can only pay attention for a couple of minutes at a time. Our subconscious is like a computer hard drive, storing all our thoughts and arranging them within the neural network of our brains, an interconnected pathway of nerves. The more often we have a thought or feeling, the stronger the connection becomes between the neurons that store the information that underlies it. So, unless you are awake and aware, most of your thoughts and actions are governed by your subconscious. **Want a different result in any area of your life? Then change your beliefs!**

This knowledge may open the door for you to understand that *most* of what you are now programmed with is someone else's limiting beliefs that are based in fear. Our beliefs are someone else's limiting thoughts! Is it time to uncover what you believe, and then to replace your limiting beliefs with new and empowering beliefs based on your ideals. The next Steps discuss the present moment, meditation, and creating powerful intentions that can start you on the path to release and replace your limiting beliefs.

> We live our lives based on what we believe about our world, ourselves, our capabilities, and our limits.
> —Gregg Braden, *The Divine Matrix*

Exploration:
- What beliefs do you share with your parents?
- Beliefs around money, health, relationships?

- How are you currently living the life of your parents at a slightly higher level?
- Would you like to live the life you decide to have?

Filters of the Belief System

The reticular activating system (RAS) is the part of your brain that notices things that are connected with your thoughts. Have you noticed that as soon as you buy a new car, you see that kind of car everywhere you go? Why does that happen all of a sudden? At any given moment, there are millions of things we could focus on anywhere: sights, sounds, smells, tastes, sensations, and the like. When you buy the new car, your brain actually filters out the other cars through the RAS so that you see the one like yours. Your brain does this with your beliefs as well. It will find evidence of them all over the place, such as online and on television. When your beliefs become more aligned with your ideals, you get a whole new perspective on life, and therefore, the things you notice will change as well.

> Everything that irritates us about others can lead us to an understanding of ourselves.
>
> —Carl Jung

Global Beliefs—Worldwide and Individual

Some beliefs are shared by most on the planet; some belief systems are shared by the citizens of the country they live in, and so on down the line to our familial units. The greater part of the beliefs we hold are someone else's. What are the global beliefs you buy into? Most of our society-wide beliefs are limiting and fear-based. Look at the current "recession" and beliefs around the economy.

Other than a small minority, the whole world believes that we are in a downturn. The idea was propagated by the media and fed to us every day for many years, pounded into our heads every day, and it continues. The media kept saying: "A recession is coming…Are we in a recession? A recession is coming…We *are* in a recession!" As a result, many bought into it, became fearful, and stopped living normally.

Did you create economic hardship in the last five to ten years? You didn't need to! There is plenty of money and opportunity as long as you *believe* there is. Could it be time for you to choose what you want to believe?

The Grandfather of Creating Your Reality

If you're new to these ideas, check out Earl Nightingale's CD program, *The Strangest Secret*, at www.Nightingale.com. It is hard to believe that these ideas and principles have been on recordings for more than fifty years! Nightingale was a pioneer in getting these messages out to the masses. His most famous quote from the *Strangest Secret* is, "You are now, and you do become, what you think about." When you study the teachings of the ancient mystics, you may find that all the information is eerily similar.

Paradigm Shifts—How to Change Your Beliefs

Beliefs are *the* most important piece of life's puzzle. Your beliefs are the only things stopping you from achieving your ideals in every aspect of your life. A paradigm shift is what you need to make your ideals a reality. When I learned this, I found that most of my beliefs were hugely limiting and preventing me from moving forward and toward what I wanted out of life.

Your beliefs become your thoughts,
Your thoughts become your words,
Your words become your actions,
Your actions become your habits,
Your habits become your values,
Your values become your destiny!
—Gandhi

Mohandas K. Gandhi, Esq

Gandhi was an attorney before he became a political and spiritual leader. This man changed the world. This man, whom some would call frail, took on one of the world's most powerful countries, and without the use of any force toppled the control the British Empire had over his country of India. Gandhi's life was anything but easy, but he found his calling as a spiritual leader and was able to achieve things that few could ever dream of. Everyone, attorneys and nonattorneys alike, should read his autobiography and see the movie based on his life.

Exploration:
- What do you believe now about money?
- Your health?
- Your relationships?

For each of these questions, a set of subquestions is laid out in a form for you to fill in below. They can begin your exploration into what is stored in your subconscious. Once you uncover what is in there, you can begin to remove what you don't want and replace it with better programming.

Pull out a notebook or some paper and just write down whatever comes into your mind immediately after reading the questions. Don't "think" about the answers. If you would like to print this exercise, the following questions can also be found online at:

http://www.RaisingTheBarBook.com/explorebeliefs

- Current Beliefs: What do you currently believe about money?

  _____
  _____
  _____

- Is it easy or hard to make money? Why?

  _____
  _____
  _____

- Do you have to work really hard to make the income you desire? Why?

  _____
  _____
  _____

- What were (or still are) your parents' beliefs about money? Do you share the beliefs? Are they limiting or not?

  _____
  _____
  _____
  _____

- What did you learn about money from the example your parents set in your childhood and beyond?

  _____
  _____
  _____

  o Did they struggle to "make ends meet"? _____

○ How do you continue the limitations of your parents by sharing their beliefs about money?

_____

_____

_____

• Did your income go down due to the "recession"? Why?

_____

_____

_____

_____

• Ideal Beliefs: What you would like to believe about money (making it, having it, saving it, and spending it)?

_____

_____

_____

_____

_____

_____

_____

• What would having more money do for and in your life?

_____

_____

Money is just a representation of energy. It is a medium of exchange used to trade for services or products. Do you know people who make money easily—who don't have to work hard for it? There are plenty of people like this. How do they do it? They don't believe the same things as people who think money is hard to come by and that you have to work your ass off for it.

Business:

- What do you believe about running a business? Is it hard or easy?

  _____

  _____

- What about your clients? What do you believe about them? Are they difficult or easy?

  _____

  _____

- What about your team members? Your boss (if you have one)?

  _____

  _____

- What is it like to attract new clients and business? Easy or difficult? Why?

  _____

  _____

  _____

- What does the ideal business and career look like to you?

  _____

  _____

Health:

- How often per week do you feel really healthy and vital?

  _____

- How many times do you get sick each year?

  _____

- How do you feel about exercise? What is it like? Why?

  _____

_____

- What is your relationship with food? Are you addicted to it? Why?

_____

_____

_____

- Do you need to lose some weight? How much?

_____

- Is it easy or hard to lose weight? Do you blame this on your genetics?

_____

_____

_____

- Do you have all the energy you need (and want) every day?

_____

- If not, why not? _____

Relationship with Significant Other:
- Are you currently in a relationship? _____
- Is being in a relationship difficult or easy? Why? Where did you learn that?

_____

_____

_____

- What does your ideal relationship look like?

_____

_____

_____

Life Purpose:

- Do you believe you have a purpose for your life? Why or why not?

  _____

  _____

  _____

- Is the career you are in now your purpose?

  _____

  _____

  _____

- What would life be like if you were doing what you really loved and had massive passion for?

  _____

  _____

  _____

- What would being a lawyer be like if you could connect or reconnect with the passion and purpose of being in the law?

  _____

  _____

  _____

- Do you believe you will find your purpose if it is not what you are doing now?

  _____

  _____

  _____

Life Balance:

- Do you think balance between your personal life and your business life is possible?

  _____

  _____

- Do you have balance in your life? Why or why not?

  _____

  _____

  _____

- Do you believe that being a lawyer means not having flow and balance in your life overall? Why or why not?

  _____

  _____

  _____

- What would your life be like if you were able to find true balance in all areas? What would it *feel* like to you?

  _____

  _____

  _____

  _____

  _____

  _____

Life in General:

- Do you think life is hard or easy? Why?

  _____

  _____

  _____

- Can life really be easy? Can you really attain all your ideals?

  _____

  _____

  _____

- What kind of lifestyle do you believe you deserve?

  _____

  _____

  _____

- What does your ideal lifestyle consist of? How many weeks off do you take per year? How many hours do you devote to your career every day?

  _____

  _____

  _____

  _____

  _____

  _____

For further exploration: Ask yourself similar questions about additional categories that apply to you, such children and family, friends, fun and recreation, personal growth, community, and any other area where you would like to know more about what you believe.

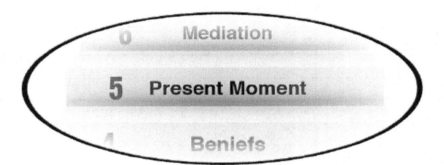

Step #5 The Present Moment
CHAPTER 11

Yesterday is history, tomorrow is a mystery, today is a gift of God, which is why we call it the present.

—Bil Keane

There is only one time that is important—now! It is the most important time because it is the only time that we have any power.

—Leo Tolstoy

The present moment is truly a gift you can choose to accept. Living in the moment is our true nature. Babies have no concept of "self" and live in the moment. Once we begin to see that we are our own being (usually toddler stage), our moment-to-moment awareness is usually focused on the past or worrying about the future. But all we really have is the present moment. The past is gone, and the future never gets here.

How much time do you spend thinking every day? If you are not living in the moment by being aware of it, your mind is like a hamster running around a wheel and getting nowhere. Can you change the past? No, that is impossible. Do you spend a lot of time worrying about the future and what *might* happen? How much of what you've worried about happening ever actually happened?

Humans love to spend time on "what-ifs" and maybes. Directing our attention in each moment allows us to focus our conscious minds for long periods. This way of being has been called consciousness, awareness, present-moment awareness, or mindfulness.

Living from the past or in the future creates the "suffering" that Buddha searched for the solution to. So much of our lives pass us unexperienced when we live in our heads. Thinking shuts out the beauty of our moment-to-moment experiences. Thinking about the past or the future is the epitome of living from the head or ego. When we live in the moment, we connect with the heart space—our intuition—and our true powers can emerge. How do we live in the moment? Simply by fully *being* in the very moment that is happening in the eternal now. Being in the "now" allows all the thinking or mind chatter to drift away.

I had never heard of being in the present moment until I read Eckhart Tolle's *The Power of Now* on the recommendation of a business coach. My life has not been the same since. The book opened me up to the reasons for living in the moment. So began my obsession with the topic, and I began to create my own framework for living in the moment. I found books, seminars, and meditations that allowed me to deeply understand living in the moment. All great masters who connected with the present moment (such as the Dalai Lama, Jesus, and Buddha) all had to condition their minds to be able to do it.

From the present moment, there is nothing but possibilities. What are the benefits of living in the now?

- You let go of worry and fear.
- You disconnect from your head.

- You gain powerful, laser-like focus on whatever you turn your attention to.
- You make huge gains in productivity, creating more free time.
- You release resistance and stress.
- You deeply connect with your intuition and heart space in every moment.
- You can truly *be with* whomever you're with or whatever you're doing.

> If you are depressed, you are living in the past. If you are anxious, you are living in the future. If you are at peace, then you are living in the present.
>
> —Lao Tzu

What if you gave your children, spouse, or even clients your *full* attention when you're with them? How would your relationships benefit in this new state of being? Be fully present wherever you are. All anyone wants from us is our attention. We usually spend many of our waking hours aimlessly thinking or worrying, but if we are in the moment, we are giving whomever we are with all of our attention. It is truly a present, a gift, to ourselves, and to anyone we spend time with.

Teach your children about being in the moment, and attention deficit disorder and similar issues aren't in their reality anymore. Attention deficit is a problem humanity shares with all other animals, but they live in the moment. The real "disorder" of our species is that we are not taught how to experience the amazing gift that is this moment. (Are you reading this paragraph with all your attention, in the moment? Or are you multitasking?)

Give whatever you are doing and whoever you are with the gift of your attention.

—Jim Rohn

Tolle's *The Power of Now* may have exposed me to the *idea* and the benefits of being in the present moment, but it left me wanting some kind of framework for learning how to really be in it. Shortly afterward, I found a book that provided the steps and framework I had been looking for: *The Presence Process: A Journey into Present Moment Awareness*, by Michael Brown. This is a must-read for anyone who would like to really learn to live life in the present.

Become the "Observer" of Your Thoughts

Have you ever stopped to listen to what you say to yourself? This may seem a strange question if you have never observed your own thoughts, but it was such a life changer for me. Observing your own thoughts is like listening to them as if they were a radio talk show. Observing what we say to ourselves and seeing how much we have allowed our minds to be programmed by others is essential for breaking free from our past programming and directing our attention to our ideals.

What do you say when you talk to yourself? There is so much negativity everywhere we look. Watching what we allow ourselves to be exposed to guards against repeated exposure to the ideas that created many of our limiting beliefs and ends up affecting our mind chatter. Most of our self-talk is judgment- and fear-based. Many teachers call self-talk "mind chatter," and it can be quite detrimental. When you observe your thoughts, you may realize that you are not your thoughts. You begin to "just be." Later, I'll show you how to use this insight as a critical part of eliminating the "blame game."

When I learned how to be an observer of my own thoughts, I couldn't believe some of the stuff I was saying to myself. Lots of self-judgment and criticism of myself and others was prevalent. Human beings are judgment machines: we judge it all, but we evaluate ourselves the harshest. But what can you appreciate about yourself? Each one of us is incredibly special and unique. Present-moment living allows us to love and appreciate ourselves more deeply every day.

> Ordinary thoughts course through our mind like a deafening waterfall.
>
> —Jon Kabat-Zinn

The Myth of Multitasking

The concept of "multitasking" has garnered a lot of attention over the past ten years or so. Being able to get more done by doing several things at once has been the focus of many articles and discussions. But does it pay to be scattered, doing many things at once? What has more impact, a laser or a light bulb? A laser beam does, since it is hundreds of beams of light superfocused in a small area, unlike the light bulb, which throws off light all over the place. Lasers are used to cut through solid metal! When you live in the moment, you fully direct all your attention onto one thing, not ten.

> The secret of health for both mind and body is not to mourn for the past, nor to worry about the future, but to live the present moment wisely and earnestly.
>
> —Buddha

Shifting Your Paradigm

When you are able to observe your thoughts and quiet them, you are entering the present moment. When you focus on anything with awareness, you are in the moment. Simple things become new again when you enter the moment and experience them. To me, being in the present moment means truly allowing myself to *experience* life as it was meant to be. So, for example, when you eat, experience it fully. Actually taste and savor the food. If you find yourself in self-talk, bring your attention to your breath.

Whenever you have a couple of minutes, try to:

- Notice and observe thoughts.
- Stop and focus your attention on your breath, heart, or any body area you choose.
- Get quiet and hold your attention on the body.
- Relax your body.
- Breathe!

The more you practice this way of being, the easier it gets, and it becomes a habit.

Intention

6 **Meditation**

Present Moment

Step #6 A Quiet Mind
CHAPTER 12

Each one has to find his peace from within. And peace to be real must be unaffected by outside circumstances.

—Gandhi

Constant, unending thinking is a disease, and it can lead to sickness and disease in the body. Taking time every day to meditate and quiet your mind has numerous benefits. A few of them are:

- Lower blood pressure and respiratory rate
- Relaxed mind and body
- Easing or elimination of muscle tension
- Better mental focus
- Deeper connection with spirit/soul/God
- Decrease in worry and restless thinking

What is meditation? At first, it is to slow down your thoughts to the point where you can direct your attention. Since we are addicted to thinking, lots of people find the act of stopping thought to be a challenge. The disease of constant thought is so ingrained in our society that many new meditators really struggle to even slow their thoughts down at all. The key is to practice! Becoming good at meditation is like anything else. The more you practice, the easier it gets. Don't judge anything about meditation sessions. Let everything progress as it needs to.

Exploration:
- Sit in a quiet room and get comfortable. Focus all your attention on your breath; follow it in and out.
- Breathe as deeply as you can, filling in your belly first, and then your chest.
- From there, you can breathe in your nose and out your nose, or in and out of your mouth. Either is OK; you choose.
- Keep all your attention on the in and out of each breath.
- If you find thoughts entering your mind, don't judge that. Just be aware that it is happening, and bring your attention back to your breath.

This is a great way to begin the practice of meditating. It's how I started. Many times during the day, if I feel some tension, I do this exercise for a quick break to relax. It is a way to bring yourself back into the present moment.

There are many different ways to meditate. Here are some of the most widely used ways to quiet one's mind and body:

1. Zen or Buddhist method. The meditator focuses attention on an object or on a specific or general part of the body. Zen meditators use various sitting positions and methods of breathing while they quiet their minds. The result is a release of attachment to the mind and of judgment.
2. Mindfulness Meditation method. The meditator focuses on the moment through attention to the in and out of breath, an area of the body, or something in the room. In the "third-eye

meditation" variant, the point between the eyebrows is used as the focus.

3. Mantra Meditation. This process involves saying a word or string of words, on the act of which all focus is placed.
4. Movement Meditation. This method focuses on the movement or positions of the body. Qi (or chi) gong and yoga are this type of meditation.
5. Walking Meditation. Thich Nhat Hanh, a Buddhist monk and teacher, has popularized this style of meditation. It involves directing all attention on the act of walking: the feeling of one's legs and feet moving and of the feet hitting the ground, and connecting it all to the breath.

I never think of the future. It comes soon enough.

—Albert Einstein

Why Don't More People Meditate?

If meditation has such amazing and profound benefits, why don't more people do it? Most of us have patterns of daily life that are hard to give up. Do you find yourself "crashing" after a long day and turning on the television? What about other ways to decompress, like drinking alcohol or eating? What is your routine for when the workday is over? Many studies have shown that habits form for anything (good or bad) we do regularly for thirty days or more. These habits become addictions that we don't like to give up.

Exploration:
• What benefits might you gain from including meditation in your life?

Start with the focus on your breath and create it as a new and empowering habit!

"In"Tense

As you probably already know, whether you are a judge, lawyer, paralegal, or legal secretary, being in the legal profession is a difficult proposition, to say the least. Before I meditated as a normal part of life, I was always tensed up. My neck and back were always knotted up, and I had headaches all the time. Even on vacation, I needed two or three days to start feeling calm and relaxed. In her book *Radical Acceptance,* Tara Brach says we are in a constant state of fear, and that "when we stop tensing against life, we open to an awareness that is immeasurably large and suffused with love." Let go and relax through a quiet mind and being in the moment. Your mind and body will thank you for it.

8   Balance

7   Intention

6   Mediation

Lawyers are quite the different breed. We believe that our codified system of laws and case law are like a branch of science where we try out different hypotheses based on our views of a case. Law is more art than science, but it doesn't stop us as a profession from having a scientific worldview. "If I can't see or feel it, then it doesn't exist" is an empirical viewpoint. But continue to have an open mind and do your best not to judge any of the following ideas. Let go of your preconceived notions about what you *think you know* reality is.

An intention or goal is something you want to create, do, have, make, experience. Simply put, it is a result you would like. In this context, you may have heard the word "goal" applied to such items, but you may not have heard "intention." Here, I use them interchangeably.

Would you like to take a trip to Paris, or buy a new car or a new house? Would you like to have ideal clients and team members and a thriving law practice that is respected in your community for doing the right thing for every client?

I have come to know that a prerequisite to manifesting in our lives begins with creating a powerful intention in regard to the things or experiences you would like to attract to your life. How do you create an intention? First, get really clear about the end result you would like. Want to create more money, a new car, more ideal clients? There is nothing at all wrong with wanting more money in your world, or anything else that supports your greater good, for that matter. Getting clear about the end result entails considering what more money, a new car, or anything else looks like in your mind's eye. I have made large chunks of money as a result of creating an intention, but what I didn't realize was that I had given no attention to what I believed about how I would make it. (I'm heading somewhere important with this, so please get in the moment!)

To get really clear about an end result, take a look at *all* your beliefs around it. For instance, creating an intention around more income has different pieces to it. For me, more money in my life used to equate to more work, and ultimately, more problems and lots of stress. Why? My belief was that I *personally* had to work harder and longer to make more money. And my belief manifested. Yes, I had more money in my bank account, but my peace of mind and health suffered as a result. So the end result I visualize now includes balance and peace of mind connected to more money in my life. The big picture is important!

Then, visualize the end result in your mind's eye as if it has already manifested in your life. While doing this, connect with the *feeling* you get. What will you *feel* like when you get your result? Connecting with this *feeling* of completion is key. When we are able to do that, it is a form of gratitude. We are thankful for the end result before it has even manifested!

It is important to allow any limiting beliefs you may have around the end result to be uncovered so that you can replace them. We can uncover many of our limiting beliefs by spending time each day simply visualizing what we would like in our lives. Chances are that during visualization, you will literally hear these limiting thoughts in your mind.

When your focus is on the end result, you are sending the universe instructions on what you want to attract. Limiting beliefs about your end result actually send the universe mixed signals. Want to make more money? Clear out your limiting ideas about making money. Want to lose weight? Let go of your beliefs around food, health, and losing weight. You get the idea. Losing weight may be quite difficult if you believe that the process is difficult and that your genetics make it inherently hard.

These processes of meditation and visualization have changed my life in innumerable ways. How? Well, I have created my ideal in every single aspect of my life, and I continue to raise the bar in them all. I used these processes to lose fifty pounds; my health and energy are amazing. I have a beautiful new, ideal house; two years' worth of expenses in the bank, amazing cars, and ideal clients. I have fully connected with and am fulfilling my life purpose, and, best of all, I have an awesome relationship with my partner in life, Candice.

Let me say a little more about this process in action in my life. In 2006, the real estate market began a downward spiral. Many people began defaulting on their mortgages as the market crashed. Property values plummeted, and the fear about buying and selling gripped the collective consciousness. As a title agent and closing attorney, I felt that business had seemed to become difficult since the number of people buying houses diminished greatly. Many of my colleagues disappeared.

Fortunately, I had already created an intention to thrive financially, regardless of the marketplace. I ended up splitting from my law and business partner of ten years to start a new law firm. I created an intention around the amount of monthly income I desired and spent time every day focusing on the end result and what it would feel like to see that amount of money in my bank account at the end of each month.

As I visualized the end result and connected with the feeling of completion, various limiting beliefs began to show themselves as questions I heard in my mind. Beliefs came up like, *How can I make money? We're in a recession, for God's sake! You have to work really hard to make that much money! Money is hard to come by; there isn't that much business right now. No one is buying or selling houses, so where are the closings going to come from?*

I was diligent at making sure to take time for my self-care routine every day. I meditated, did yoga, and exercised. Distractions can have a definite impact on whether we choose to care for ourselves physically. I found that adding daily reminders helped me not to get caught up in the myriad other things I could spend my free time on. Once I had been meditating every day for several months, it became a habit. You may find, as I did, that once something you actually want to do becomes a habit, you will make sure you sit and get quiet every day, regardless of the adversity you may find in any day.

When I was done with my routine, having sufficiently relaxed my mind and body and visualized my ideal outcome, I would sit in front of my computer and see my bank deposits adding up to the amount I had intended. As the days passed, my limiting thoughts were getting smaller and weaker, and my ability to connect with the all-important feeling of having the income was becoming very real. In a couple of months, the amount of money I had been visualizing had manifested. And it continues every month. The feeling of witnessing this manifestation was amazing.

Use this process for any intention, but keep in mind that the end result should always be for the greater good. I always teach others that when choosing an end result, it is a good idea to reach for one that is somewhat of a stretch from their current situation. This allows many limiting beliefs to bubble up from the subconscious mind. So, for instance, if you want to create more money in your life, pick a number that is a little difficult for your brain to "think" you can attain. As the days pass, you should be able to connect with the feeling of completion a bit more, and you will let go of the limiters more and more.

Framework for Creating Intentions

1. Make sure the result you are looking for is for your highest and best!
2. Get clear about what your end result looks like by creating a detail-rich view of the ideal.
3. Visualize the end result as if it were already there, and connect with the feeling you get that it is.
4. Let go of and release any worn-out and limiting beliefs around the intention.
5. Start to take action on the inspiration that your intuition provides you.

As you create your intentions, listen to your intuition. It will guide you in the direction of your ideal. You begin to attract the right people, places, and things. You cannot lock yourself in your house and expect things to happen. Start taking small steps toward reaching your goals! The amazing thing about creating intentions is the unlimited possibility that any intention holds within it. Anything can happen! This Step is the cornerstone of creating your new and ideal life.

> The great secret about goals and visions is not the future they describe but the change in the present they engender.
> —David Allen

Act As If

The idea to "act as if" came to me years ago. I made the decision to start living my life "as if" all my intentions were already a reality. This way of thinking and being requires a shift in your beliefs and then small steps toward your intentions. Take the first step, and your pathway becomes illuminated. The next step does the same, and so on. If you never take the first step, you have *no* chance of ever achieving what you desire.

The existence of this book is a good example of this principle in action. The conception of it came to me a few years ago. I knew such a book could really make a difference. Even though I was a practicing lawyer and had spent nineteen years in school doing required educational writing, I had never written a book. There were so many unknowns to the process, so many questions, and I had no idea where to find answers. Fear held me back for a short time, but then I just decided to take action on what my intuition was guiding me toward. I used my favorite mind-mapping software to start the process. The ideas flowed so quickly that my typing couldn't keep up! As I worked, I found the next steps were always illuminated with the answers I needed, books I needed to read, and seminars that lit the way toward completion.

Exploration:

- What is one big goal you have had for a while?
- What one thing could you do today to get things moving along? Get some mind-mapping software and start to brainstorm your big idea.

Releasing the Lack

So we've considered how the mass consciousness of the "recession" led to widespread problems. There were many reasons for it, but I've pointed my finger mainly at the media and how they sensationalized the issue, causing billions around the world to believe in an economic downturn. It will continue until you and I decide to change our thoughts about it.

Exploration:

- Have you bought into the idea of scarcity?
- Have you let it affect your business and income?
- Are these beliefs limiting or expanding?
- Is it time to reach for more empowering beliefs about prosperity?

Doubts

There's a story about a new farmer who dug some trenches to plant his seeds. He plopped some in every couple of inches and covered them all up. He then added water and watched his field for the next couple of weeks. He kept adding water and watching, waiting for the sprouts to emerge. He grew impatient and dug at the ground with a shovel. When he stopped his ranting and raving, he looked down and saw that the seeds had actually sprouted but had not yet pushed up through the earth. He was unable to believe in progress because he just could not see it happening. So what's the moral of this story?

You plant the seeds of your intentions with meditation and visualization. It takes some time for your crops—results—to germinate and become sprouts of what will eventually be your fruit (your ideal outcome). Don't give up on your intentions because you don't see instant results. Some intentions may be easy to work with and may produce results quickly, but others require the release of lots of limiting thoughts associated with your desired end result. It all depends on your beliefs!

We think that just because we create an intention and visualize the end result, we will get results instantaneously! Our society is addicted to instant gratification. We can find fast food any time of day in most cities, grocery stores are at our beck and call, and we can order stuff online and have it in our hands the very next day. But that's not how everything works. When you set the wheels in motion, it is important to have faith, trust, and believe.

Have Faith, Trust, and Believe

Years ago, I wrote

"Faith—Trust—Believe"

on the whiteboard in my office. Why?

I had the same issues with instant gratification I mentioned. I desired my intentions to materialize quickly, and in the exact fashion I believed they should. I decided to focus and visualize until the end results appeared, no matter the time it took. So for me, those three words said it all.

Have complete **FAITH** in your ability to create your intentions.
TRUST that whatever you put your attention on is coming to you once you are able to release your limitations, and
BELIEVE with all your being that the end result will manifest.

There is an important piece you must not miss here: any limitation you have placed on the end result needs to be let go of and released. I like to think of our ideals as wine in a bottle, and the limitations we place on them as the cork. With your cork stuck securely in an amazing bottle of wine, you don't allow your ideals to flow to you. Until you release the cork, you keep your intentions waiting and contained. Use the framework of meditation and visualization as your corkscrew. Let go of limiting beliefs that are standing in the way. When Michelangelo was ready to chip away at a large block of stone to create what we now know as *David*, he said that he could "see" *David* inside before he even began. Each of our intentions is like a big block of marble, ready for us to chisel away what doesn't belong and make it into our own *David* masterpiece.

As you create your intentions and visualize the end result with feeling, the right people, places, and things will be attracted into your reality, and your intuition will alert you to the next steps on your path to the end result as long as you allow its messages to come through and you listen to them.

Your Ideal Life

You have the right to live the life you've dreamed of. To wake up to it requires that you examine your life, what you believe, and what your brain has been "programmed" with over the years.

Beginning to craft your ideals can start with looking at where you are presently. What is working and what isn't? Acceptance of where you are right now is part of this process. Any time I want to create an ideal, whether it be a client, a new team member, or even better health, my starting place is to accept what is and let go of the judgments about it. However, sometimes we also need to look to our pasts to compare what we didn't like about it that led us to create what we have now. Then, from the present, we can craft the ideal and what it looks like in our mind's eye. How would we know what is ideal for us if we hadn't experienced what wasn't? Then we get *really clear* about the end result we seek. Then we factor in balance and a nice rhythm to life, with plenty of time for family, rest, and relaxation.

Personally, my ideals have changed dramatically since I was in college. I wanted what most Americans do: the American dream. It's full of possessions, a huge house, a five-car garage to hold many sports cars, and rooms filled with stuff, much of which we'll never use. Over the years, I've had the BMW, the Cadillacs, and the toys, but as my life progressed, I found that these things didn't really matter to me anymore. Yes, I still have preferences, but the desire for money does not rule me as it once did. Now it has become more about what I can do with my earnings to help others, animals, and the world. This change happens when you shift from the head to the heart.

Our society is caught up in the ego, which craves possessions and more stuff. The ego thinks that the more stuff we have, the happier we will be. It is all empty, and stuff begins to be a burden very quickly. The bigger the house, the more upkeep; the more cars...Well, you get the point. Many Americans are now beginning to downsize. You may find that when you know your life purpose, you will stop the endless search for the next purchase and start to really live your life. We know that many lawyers get into the business because they want the American dream and the money, but it does come with a price. Our country is paying it in a huge way.

Exploration:
- What does your *ideal* life look like in your mind's eye?
- How much money do you make in your ideal life?
- What does your relationship with your significant other and family look like when you picture the ideal?
- Do you work less and spend time with those who really matter to you?
- How many weeks of vacation do you take a year?
- What kind of health do you enjoy as your ideal self?

> You can have everything in life you want if you'll just help enough other people get what they want.
>
> —Zig Ziglar

Attachment to an Outcome

Sometimes we want a goal so badly that we become attached to it. Being attached to an outcome is a state of being in which you feel as if you can't live without it and spend lots of time wondering why you don't have it yet. The issue with being attached to anything in this life is that you actually repel it. How? When this mind-set has hold of you, your attention is actually on *not having* what you want. This is how so many people with no money stay stuck. They "need" money, so all they think about is that they don't have any! It is a vicious circle that many cannot find a way out of. Most will get what they absolutely need to pay their bills, but they never get any more.

If you find yourself attached to the outcome of an intention, let it go and just focus on the end result. Really connect with the *feeling* of it being true. The process of manifesting the end result will be as short or long as it takes to release your attachment and, of course, your limiting beliefs!

The "Cursed Hows" and Surrendering the Outcome

When we create an intention about an outcome we would like, we immediately want to know how, where, and when it will manifest. Teacher and author Mike Dooley calls this common issue the "cursed hows." Questions that may pop up when we visualize can include "How is this going to happen," or "Where will the money come from?" This is a form of attachment to the outcome. Dooley suggests that we let go of any need to know *how* and let the universe do as it sees fit. Just have faith, trust, and believe, and let it all play out just as it needs to. Surrender all of your preconceived notions around how long something should take, how it will happen, or who may be part of the end result. Surrendering entails letting all of the details line up the way they need to and a complete trust in the process. Do your visualizations and let it go! Get out of the way and let the universe do its job.

Affirmations

Do affirmations work? Many self-improvement authors and speakers seem to swear by them. Affirmations are statements in the positive about something you want, do, or have, such as, "I am rich and money comes to me quickly" or "I have perfect health and all my issues have disappeared." If you have read any kind of self-help book over the past thirty years, chances are you have tried them. Do they work?

My experience of affirmations is that they are attempts to talk oneself into something without allowing new beliefs to replace old ones. Said another way, affirmations are like throwing fresh apples on top of a pile of rotten ones, thinking that the whole pile will be suddenly fresh again. The affirmation process usually takes a long time to work (if ever), and I see that most just get frustrated with it and stop doing it (myself included). What many teachings on affirmations miss is the connection to the feeling of the end result being manifested.

As you now know, your subconscious is where all your beliefs reside. Whether they are empowering or disempowering beliefs is a result of your judgment. *Understand for now that nothing is good or bad until we make it so.* Without uncovering and replacing your limiting beliefs, the mechanical repetition of statements doesn't have much power to create what you want. You can think about what you would like every minute of every day, but if you have beliefs that contradict your ideal outcome, change is not likely to happen. Affirmations can be powerful when coupled with the feeling of the end result already accomplished, so feel the feeling of accomplishment when saying them.

Old Beliefs Out, New Beliefs In

My own routine for creating the ideal has been part of my life for almost ten years now, in different iterations. Here it is in a nice, easy-to-integrate framework. I hope you use it to change your life. It sure changed mine!

A Simple Daily Framework to Create Your Ideals

Here's my easy, daily step-by-step process. Put your own spin on it if you like. Just keep doing it; after a short while, it becomes a habit—the kind of habit you want.

Get comfortable and close your eyes. Get into the present moment, focusing all your attention on your breath. Be fully aware of each in and out of your breath. Keep breathing deeply until you get into a restful and relaxed state. Don't be concerned about how long it takes you to get into this relaxed state.

Once you feel very relaxed and peaceful, spend time focusing on the intentions you have created: in your mind's eye, picture the end result you want to bring into your life. Get as graphic as you can in your visualization. Make it *feel* as real as you can.

Feel what it feels like to have already created the end result of the intention.

As you now know, the feeling is the key here. It is really what you want when you desire anything: the feeling that it gives you! When you connect with the completion of it all, you are actually putting your mind into a state of deep gratitude for the end result you want.

This framework is a very powerful way to either start or end your day. I usually end my day with it, since I like to sleep afterward (releasing the stress from the day and quieting the mind is a great segue into a deep and restful sleep!). It is a good idea to make sure you have plenty of time to complete the routine, since you don't want to be rushed.

For some more information on visualizations, see *Creative Visualization* by Shakti Gawain.

What would you like to have, do, be, create, explore, enjoy, or develop in your life? Not all intentions are about money. What about all the other areas of your life besides your finances? What would you like in these areas of your life?

- Family and friends
- Spouse/significant other/life partner—what kind of relationship do you want?
- Home/physical environment
- Automobile
- Health and vibrancy
- Spirituality and connection with your source/soul
- Ideal career
- Ideal clients/ideal team members
- Office environment
- Vacations and time off

Get visualizing!

Purpose & Choice
CHAPTER 14

The millions are awake enough for physical labor. But only one in a million is awake enough for effective intellectual exertions, only one in a hundred million to poetic or divine life. To be awake is to be alive. I have never yet met a man who was quite awake. How could I have looked him in the face?

—Henry David Thoreau, *Walden*

Living with Purpose

So far, you have learned how to begin to live in the present moment, how to release and replace limiting beliefs with new and empowering ones, and how to visualize. This is all part of waking up, of being aware and truly *alive*!

Question everything, and replace the disempowering with the empowering! When we have a purpose in and for our lives, we connect with life in a much deeper way. Things get brighter, and as we live in the moment more and more, our lives get more meaningful. We all have choices in every moment of every day. We can go from limited habits to rituals that create more wealth, vitality, greater good for all, and best of all, a joy-filled existence.

The next couple of sections explore some ways that we can choose how to feel about anything and uncover old, worn-out patterns that we may have run for most of our lives. Then we will look at how we can be proactive instead of reactive to life.

The Moment of Choice

Did you know that you have a choice when you make any decision? Any decision, big or small, can be made from either your intuition *or* your ego. Most choices we make are split-second *reactions* ("re-action" can mean an action based on our past programming). Further, we may choose the same things over and over, regardless of whether what we choose truly benefits our lives. You usually eat the same things, watch the same TV shows, and react the same way to circumstances in your life.

You have the ability to break these patterns. Wouldn't it be empowering to *consciously* make a choice each time instead of just unconsciously *re*-acting?

> The unexamined life is not worth living.
>
> —Socrates

Breaking Unwanted Patterns

We all have habits and patterns that end up creating our outcomes and our lives. Habits and patterns are just strings of thoughts that you or others have programmed your subconscious mind with over and over again. Are you aware of the habits and patterns you currently follow? Chances are, you don't know what they are, or why.

Addictions are a perfect example of behavior that is created by patterns. Every time addicts give in to the addiction, they may have the same feelings and say the same things to themselves. Patterns and habits apply to all of our behaviors and decisions, large or small.

122

A common excuse is, "Oh, I'll do it later today," and then "I'm tired today...definitely tomorrow!" Do you do that? (I know I've been guilty of it, time and time again.)

Awareness allows you to break such patterns by recognizing them as they happen so you can make a different choice in the moment. The power in living in the moment and observing your thoughts is the ability to literally change your mind when you recognize habitual choices. Recognition ends the reactivity and can lead you to new and more empowering choices.

Let's look at this even deeper. Do you find yourself reacting similarly in similar situations? When you react, you are in effect acting in the same way as you did in the past. To be proactive is to provide a response in the moment without allowing past conditioning to influence an action or decision. When our actions are only reactions, we are on autopilot, giving ourselves no opportunity to make a different or better choice. Take a moment before you react to anything and give yourself a chance to create the kind of response you deem best in the situation. Your response might be quite different if you give yourself a few seconds while in the moment (or to get in the moment) and choose from awareness.

Since we are the creators of our own realities, we have a choice of how to respond to any thought we have. A belief is just a thought you choose to think more than once. Choose a better thought!

Exploration:
- Are there behaviors you would like to put an end to? Procrastination, addictions, and limiting thoughts are tops on most people's lists. Journal the thoughts and patterns as you discover them. If you are diligent, you can replace the

limiting thoughts with more empowering ones in the moment.

Never forget: Each belief and every thought add up to what becomes our ultimate reality.

> Every time you are tempted to react in the same old way, ask if you want to be a prisoner of the past or a pioneer of the future.
> —Deepak Chopra

Personal Responsibility

> My belief is that personal freedom cannot grow beyond personal responsibility. The more people that learn to be fully accountable for their lives, the more freedom each of us can enjoy and the more fulfilling all of our lives will be.
> —Ross Parmenter

Let's talk about society, greed, and decision making. What have your decisions been like? How do you think we are doing as a profession, or as a society? You may have noticed a distinct change in the quality of decisions that people have been making over the past couple of decades. Compare news stories from newspapers and the Internet to those from forty years ago and note the differences. Society's moral compass seems to have eroded to an all-time low quality, and it's still going down. It is up to each of us to reverse this course by taking into account our own responsibility for the issues we've all created on this planet.

When we make a choice that we know is not for the highest good (because feedback from our intuition tells us that), the next time we are faced with the same decision, it gets easier to keep choosing the same answer. When an attorney agrees to represent a client but makes the decision based on greed, the next decision based solely on monetary gain becomes easier, and even the norm.

Greed-based decision making is pervasive all over the world now. The legal profession is steeped in it, but so are all professions. Banking, accounting, medicine, and corporate business are all affected by it. How can we as individuals help to make this better? We can start with our own decisions. We can live from the heart and make choices based on how they *feel*. If the choice feels good, then do it; if it feels uncomfortable or even flat-out bad, then don't! Second, we can hold our government and corporations accountable for their decisions. Find a local bank that cares about its employees and customers and is not all about profit. This goes for all businesses. You and your family are deeply impacted by your daily decisions. Isn't it time to change how we do things?

The crux of this matter is how we can all take full responsibility for our thoughts, choices, and actions. If we want to create a better profession, society, culture, and world, it must start with each of us, *within* each of us.

The "Blame Game"

In the "blame game," we point fingers at others instead of taking full responsibility for our part in any accident, problem, dispute, or argument. Personal injury law, criminal law, and most types of civil litigation cannot function without all parties playing it at once.

Our egos want to deflect responsibility, which is natural for children to do when they're called out on mistakes or misdeeds. When a parent or teacher reprimanded you, was your initial reaction to completely deny what you did or blame someone else? The unfortunate thing is that we don't grow up anymore. We use this behavior as adults and think it is the norm.

Do you believe you create your reality? I have come to wholeheartedly agree—to know—that I draw in and attract everything that happens in my life, moment to moment. If you still don't think this is the case for you, then focus on anything that's happened in your life and see what corresponding belief you have in your subconscious that *manifested* it.

The next time you have a disagreement with someone, see if you are able to take 100 percent responsibility for your part in it. Then release any negative feelings you have about the situation. You can do this by actually experiencing the feelings you have created in reacting to the "problem." In many instances, this is all you need to create a resolution! How does this work? Since the universe is energy and information, when we judge anything, we create an emotion and feeling in the body. The feeling associated with negative judgment is usually heavy and dense. You can actually feel its weight in your body and can hold the problem in limbo or make it worse. And since what you focus your attention on grows, anytime you create resistance, you hold in the problems!

What shape would the world be in right now if we all took responsibility for everything in our lives? You might think that these ideals are "out there" and forever unattainable. But there are infinite possibilities to anything we desire to bring to our realities.

Are You Right, or Am I?

How can you ever prove you are "right" about anything? The more I have pondered this question over the years, the more it has intrigued me. There are very few real knowns in the universe. All each of us has is an opinion. We form opinions based on our beliefs, and as we now know, our beliefs are not usually our own, but inherited or learned.

Opinions can also arise from preferences we form along the path of life. Say for instance that you like a certain brand of cleaner. Your opinion is that the cleaner is the best of the bunch based on your experience with it, so you form a preference for it. This can apply to almost anything from the car we drive to the neighborhood we live in.

So, breaking it down: as a culture, what we think we're "right" about is only based on our opinions. Since others have different opinions, we see them as "wrong" or faulty.

> When you think everything is someone else's fault you will suffer a lot. When you realize that everything springs only from yourself, you will learn both peace and joy.
>
> —Dalai Lama

Case Study

As a case study, let's look at elections. These days, everywhere you look, one side bashes the other. After the 2012 US presidential election, it was pretty ugly too. People were saying how stupid some were for voting for one candidate or the other. The funny thing about elections is how very similar both candidates can be. We don't recognize this, or any similarities between the two sides, because of the perceptions and beliefs we hold in our subconscious. How do any of us really know we are "right"? Further, how can we say anyone else is "wrong" for their views? Hate to break it to you, but no one is right or wrong.

We are *all* entitled to our own opinions and beliefs, no matter how different they are from what others say. This country was founded on the idea that we all have *inalienable* rights to believe what we each *choose* to. The extreme polarity that divides our country and the world today is a result of every person thinking that they are right and everyone else is wrong. As we begin to embrace one another and our different beliefs, we can begin to heal the rifts and the wounds that have been created over thousands of years.

> It helps to remember that everyone is doing their best from their level of consciousness.
>
> —Deepak Chopra

Paradigm Shifting

If no one is ever "right," then it becomes easier to understand our fellow human beings and why they do what they do. Step into others' shoes and see if you can understand where they are coming from. What are their beliefs, judgments about you, and preferences? This "I am right, you are wrong" mentality is the reason for conflict, lawsuits, and violence in the world.

So what do you need to be able to integrate this practice into your life? It's simple. Each day, be more accommodating to the point of view of others, and see if you can understand it. As you practice this principle, it gets easier to see why others behave the way they do, and it becomes easier to work toward a solution to any problem with anyone. When it comes down to it, you are not "right," and neither are they, so let's respect one another! Remember, we are all interconnected.

Taking Responsibility

We have blamed everyone and everything else for our personal and social issues. It is time to walk the path of taking 100 percent responsibility for our actions and our decisions. Our lives are our own, and we do have a choice how to live them.

Our Many Masks

Don't let your struggle become your identity.

—Ralston Bowles

In ancient Latin, *persona* was the word for "theatrical mask." Living on purpose begets looking at other ways that we may be on automatic or autopilot, or flat-out unconscious. If you want to become the real you, then it is time to lose the masks you have been wearing with others and let the authentic you shine.

We have lived as actors in our own lives. We put on different masks for the ways we want to be perceived. You have a different persona with your spouse and with your best friend, your clients, parents, or kids. And you treat everyone differently. It is as if you were schizophrenic, on a constant roller coaster of "who do I want to be now?" Be *you*, no matter what. My intention is to be honest and open with everyone I meet, and since I am a bit of a ball buster, that's the way I am with everyone.

Exploration:
- What kinds of masks do you wear with others? Be present and see how you are with your spouse, your coworkers, or kids.
- How are you not being real and honest with them all?
- How can you get *real* with everyone?

Thinking = Judgment

We keep digging deeper and deeper into how we formulate decisions, how our beliefs are the backbone of our choices, and how perceptions rule our experiences. Our next level of exploration is into judgment and judging.

Simply put, human beings are judgment machines. We are taught to judge almost everything we see, hear, feel, taste, and touch. There are teachings that tout not being judgmental at all, but that's almost impossible. However, being in the present moment can allow us to be far less so. Knowing that we are conditioned to be in a judgmental state of mind can also help us let go of it. Being *aware* releases judgment.

What is judgment? It is the set of our individual perceptions and beliefs about life and what we think is good, bad, or neutral. Is it wrong to judge? Nothing is good or bad until we create a judgment about it! It is truly a paradox, since there really is nothing good or bad until we make it so by placing a label on it. Perception is in the eye of the beholder, and the act of judging is just resistance to what is.

The ego's job is to protect, and in the process, it creates a separation between us and others. Ego uses judgment to create a feeling of superiority or differentiation from everyone else. We are not separate, even though it may seem like we are. Quantum physics shows that we are interconnected. When you judge others, you are judging the part of yourself that you resist (remember, the world is our mirror).

Exploration:
- When was the last time you judged someone?
- When was the last time you judged anything?
- How many times did you judge what you read in the last paragraph (or anything you've read in this book)?
- Is judging others empowering or disempowering? How does judging others make you feel?
- Does this kind of thought serve your expansion in life?

- When was the last time someone else judged you?
- How did that feel?

Worst Enemy or Best Friend?

Spiritual teacher Hans King calls our constant self-talk "mind chatter." It's our ego doing all the speaking. Mind chatter can be our worst enemy, since most of it tends to be self-judgment. It's just another example of living in the head and not the heart.

We beat ourselves up day in, day out. We usually reserve the absolute worst judgments for ourselves. It is unfortunate that what we say to ourselves is usually worse than anything we've ever said to another human being. It is time to put a stop to this senselessness.

Exploration:
- What do you spend most of your mind chatter on?
- Is there a script you run in your mind? If so, what can you do to interrupt these thoughts?

Get in the moment!

Isn't it about time that we accept ourselves? Once we can get into a place of acceptance, we can then grow to appreciate and love ourselves. We all perceive faults in ourselves, and there may be things we don't like about the way we look or our ways of being. It is all just judgment! All of us, in our own ways, have amazing strengths and talents. Each of us is like no other being in the universe. Aligning with every part of our being, good or bad (remember that those are just perceptions), is the way to becoming our own best friends. Observing the judgment on the "bad" and letting it go allows you to move quickly toward your ideal life.

Meditation can be a great time to give yourself some love and appreciation!

Exploration:

Close your eyes and take some deep breaths. Relax into your chair. Spend a few minutes quieting your mind. There is so much good in each of us that we usually don't even recognize, even though so many others see it.

- What can you appreciate about yourself?
- What would you like to incorporate into your being?
- Maybe more love, honesty, or integrity?

Can you picture yourself as an infant? Hold your infant self in your arms and send you some love. Then imagine yourself at various stages of your life, and do the same thing. Send you some love, ever the while releasing any judgment or difficulties you remember from those times. This is a great way to release judgment and negativity from your past.

If you can't love yourself, how can you *truly* love anyone else? Start within, and the whole world shifts as you do. When you love yourself, you allow others to love you at an amazingly deep and profound level. How can you find ways to love and appreciate *you* more each day?

Simple kindness to one's self and all that lives is the most powerful transformational force of all.

—Dr. David R. Hawkins

9   Emotions

8   Balance

7   Intention

Step #8 A Life in Balance
CHAPTER 15

The human race is a monotonous affair. Most people spend the greatest part of their time working in order to live, and what little freedom remains so fills them with fear that they seek out any and every means to be rid of it.

—Johann Wolfgang von Goethe

Whether lawyers or not, balance in life is something most of us lack. Meditation has been key for me in keeping my life in a balanced state. In any day, there is opportunity to take some time for yourself. You just need to plan it. Schedule it if you must!

Having balance is not just about taking time off, but how you spend your time in each twenty-four-hour day. I have coached a number of people over the years. Most have given excuses for why they didn't have balance in their lives. You probably use the same ones: too many things to do, the kids have activities, or just that there is no time at the end of the day.

Life balance is essential to living from the heart space. Your ego enjoys both the status quo and drama. It will fill your mind full of "you need to do this" or "shouldn't you be doing X or Y." If you aren't living in the moment, your ego will run you all over. I won't go too deeply into this principle, though I could write a whole book on this topic (I have it in mind). I just want you to take a look at how you are living and what you are prioritizing.

Exploration:

Download the PDF chart at www.raisingthebarbook.com/ wheel and rank yourself from failing miserably (1) to experiencing your ideal (10) in each of the main areas of your life. Connect each number you've marked to the one on the next line, all the way around.

- If this were a wheel on your car or bike, how would it roll?
- Was your wheel off balance? Where are your strong and weak points? This is a great self-assessment that I use quite often.

Balance is not just about taking time off, but also about connecting with nature and getting outdoors. As a nation (and world, for that matter) we have shut ourselves off from Mother Nature. Take some time every week and go for a walk. Take your kids and animal companions (if you have them) out more often. You may notice that the more you do this, the more grounded and balanced you become.

Productivity

It is quite difficult to be in some degree of balance if you don't have your life in order in both your business and your personal lives. Things really changed in my life once I read David Allen's *Getting Things Done*. I found it to be one of the best books ever written on life management. I devoured it many years ago and have continuously implemented its principles. My productivity went through the roof, and I got extremely organized. I knew that if I wanted to attain my ideals, I had a real need for a balanced and organized lifestyle, both personally and professionally.

One of Allen's amazing ideas is that of doing "brain dumps"— gathering all of the to-dos and projects in your life, from the large to the very small tasks. Take a notebook or computer, go through your work life, and get it all down. Then walk around your house and write down each and every item you think needs to be done. Organize this stuff as you see fit, but of utmost importance is to get it all out of your head and down somewhere so you can begin to organize it all. Once the list is organized, you can accomplish the stuff or not, but the point is that your mind doesn't need to hold all this or keep reminding you what *it* thinks you need to do. What do you do with all the stuff from a brain dump or a brainstorming session? Search for free mind-mapping programs online (or use a free trial) to help you get it all organized and expanded. (I use iMindMap,‡‡‡‡ which is software from the creator of mind mapping, Tony Buzan.)

Before I integrated this brain dump into my process, every time I walked by something in the house that "needed" to be done, a thought would pop up in my mind. This kind of stuff zaps your energy! Allen's book can help you get every area of your world organized and have a lot more time to focus on the more important things.

Unleashing Your Creativity

The law profession does little to foster the creativity that we all possess. It's all about precedent, case law, and transactions, most of which are very similar. Science teaches that the left brain is used for

---

‡‡‡‡ http://www.thinkbuzan.com/

logic, math, science, language, and analytical thinking. The right brain is for music, creativity, artistic ability such as painting and poetry, expressing emotions, and most important, in my opinion, intuition. (For more information on the differences and an interesting test, see the website run by Middle Tennessee State University.§§§§) I would wager that most lawyers are left-brain dominant.

I've been more in the middle since I was a child, not really being left- or right-brain dominant, but over the past five years, I've explored more creativity in my everyday life. I purchased a sketchpad and learned more about drawing. I read about ways to connect with my right brain, which in turn led me to explore different modalities that included writing for fun and for business.

Mind mapping has many uses other than just for organizing. I use mind maps almost every day. They are amazing tools for studying and recalling information and for planning just about anything, including marketing, litigation, and travel. I used a mind map to plan out this book, and it was instrumental in the writing as well.

Why are such "maps" so powerful? They use both halves of your brain at the same time! The mind map itself is set up and modeled after the brain's neural networks and has a structure similar to that of many in nature, such as the branches of a tree.

The left side of the brain can connect with the logistical aspects of how a mind map is presented, and adding pictures and color to represent ideas connects with the right side. If you ever attend one of my live events, you will see me presenting much of my information with mind maps.

---

§§§§ http://capone.mtsu.edu/studskl/hd/LRBrain.html
The test is at http://capone.mtsu.edu/studskl/hd/hemispheric_dominance.html

Journaling

I use a Moleskine notebook to journal, but you can use a computer too. I use journaling for brainstorming; exploration; writing books, articles, and white papers; or just for fun.

There are a few ways to journal effectively. The first way I use is to write down ideas I have during the day. Many times in the past when I found myself with a great idea, I didn't write it down, and alas, the great idea was gone, possibly never to return. So I keep a journal open on my desk and bring it with me when I am out of the office. I also use Evernote (www.evernote.com) to record ideas. This software syncs with all your devices so you can access your notes from anywhere, even when you don't have an Internet connection. (Or, you can just use the online version.) I also use both my journal and Evernote to take notes on books I read.

Another interesting way to journal is called "automatic writing" or "stream of consciousness" and I use this method in a few different ways. One is to explore ideas, such as how to increase business or how to lose weight. You write the idea at the top of the page and get into the present moment, maybe by taking some deep breaths to clear your mind. Then just write down everything that comes to you about that idea. If nothing relevant comes up, don't fret; just write whatever does come to you and see what happens.

Write until the ideas stop flowing, or you decide you are done. Get as many of your ideas and thoughts down as you can. Use shorthand if you need to. My thoughts usually appear much faster than my ability to write them all down. There's also the option of using your smartphone or computer to record your thoughts in Evernote and have the recording transcribed later.

The second way to use "automatic" writing is just to get present with no agenda, writing down anything that flows into your mind. Lots of great ideas and some deep thoughts have come forth in this kind of journaling. Many sections of this book have been written using these strategies.

Distraction

The life of a lawyer is quite different today from what it was ten or twenty years ago. Instead of sorting through mail, which arrived once a day, we deal with a constant barrage of e-mails. Our cell phones allow the world to access us anytime anyone chooses, and life has become one distraction after another. As a society, we are addicted to our cell phones, e-mail, and social media. So much can sidetrack us from what we want to accomplish.

How much time do you spend every day in "distraction mode"? You may be amazed when you count up the hours each week. Many Americans spend upward of four or more hours per day watching television, surfing the Internet, and checking e-mail and social media. *Four* hours or more per day! Do people really have to wonder why they think they don't have enough time in the day?

A truly worthless distraction is watching or reading "the news," which is mostly negative, sensationalized crap. Why should we subject ourselves to a constant barrage of negativity? No, thanks. I will create my own reality based on my own ideals, not what the media wants me to program my mind with. It is *all* someone else's agenda.

Dean Jackson, a marketing teacher, explains how we get caught in the "distraction loop." We get into one many times each day at work. I found this to be true in my own life. We get to work, and the first thing we do is check e-mail, which leads into watching videos from friends, surfing the Internet, checking social media, watching more videos...then repeat. Is a loop like this part of your day? If so, it is time to break this cycle of wasted time. How much more time would you have in your day if you put an end to the loop?

What are some ways to avoid participation in the cycle of wasted time? Schedule time to close your office door and turn off your e-mail and cell. Don't allow any calls through your phone system, quiet your mind, and jump into a project or something that needs attention. Some like to get into the office early for this. When this time is blocked out and you are able to focus all your attention, it means getting a huge amount done in a relatively short time. What more could you get done every day (and every week) if you allowed this solution to be part of your routine?

Pick up a book that can help you to open and expand. Sign up for a workshop, do an online course, check out some informative videos. Take out your journal, quiet your mind, and focus.

Ending the Addiction to Television

People set aside large portions of their lives to watch a flickering box—for hours every day. They rely on the box for most of their information about the way the world is, how their politicians are behaving, and what reality is, even though the contents of the box are controlled by a handful of corporations (many of which are also in the businesses of weapons, tobacco, and alcohol). Our citizens wake up to this drug, consume it whenever possible during the day, and go to sleep with it. Many even take it with their meals.

The average American watches somewhere around thirty-four hours of television per week.***** Over a one-year span, this amounts

---

***** http://www.nielsen.com/us/en/newswire/2012/report-how-americans-are-spending-their-media-time-and-money.html to 1,768 hours, and over a typical lifetime, it equals fourteen years just watching television!

Most people's major life regrets are not about the things they've done, but about the things they've not done: the goals they never reached, the type of lover or friend or parent they wished they'd been but know they failed to be. Yet our culture encourages us to sit in front of a flickering box for dozens (at least) of hours per week, hundreds to thousands of hours a year, and thereby watch, as if from a distance, the times of our lives flow through our hands like dry sand.

If you were to reduce your television watching by half, you would have more than enough time to exercise, read, and move toward what you want from life. What could you accomplish by taking back these wasted hours of television watching or Internet surfing?

Tolerations

What are you tolerating in your life? Tolerations are things that have an open loop that needs to start or to be acted on to completion. They can be simple things, such as getting something fixed or dropping off your dry cleaning, or large projects that you have been putting off and procrastinating on. Tolerations literally drain your energy (even the little stuff does), which in turn limits the balance you can have in your life. Items many of us typically tolerate include:

- Employees showing up late
- Team members' unacceptable level of customer service
- Broken promises to ourselves and our family members
- Being late to functions and appointments

142

- Broken household items
- Grocery shopping

What are you tolerating? What solutions can you implement and move items toward completion today?

Health

> Every human being is the author of his own health or disease.
>
> —Buddha

Did you know that the energy drink industry sells *billions* of dollars in product per year? Better health, more energy, and vitality are common goals for all. Everywhere you look, someone is trying to sell you something for health, losing weight, and the like. After years of study and testing, I've found that the only thing that has ever worked for me was incorporating more fresh fruit and vegetables into my diet. The more raw fruit and vegetables, the better I feel, and the more energy I have.

All the coffee, energy drinks, or stimulants out there cannot give you the energy and health that eating better can give. These drinks are "quick fixes," empty calories, and usually made up of toxins and caffeine. How do any of us expect to thrive and be balanced if we're eating crap and sitting around on our couches? When you combine eating healthier with a moderate amount of exercise, your body moves into homeostasis and balance. When you create amazing health, the by-product is a lot of energy.

Find your equilibrium: get enough rest, quiet your mind each day, eat healthier, make exercise a priority, and create your intentions and ideals. Honor your individuality and work toward being in balance by focusing on what you feel is best for you. For instance, some of us need more sleep than others, and we thrive on different types of foods.

Exploration:
- How have you been treating your body? As a temple or a trash bin?
- What needs to change for your life to be in balance?
- What are your food choices like? Does the food you eat support your ideal lifestyle and the energy level you want?

Routine: The Rhythm and Flow of Your Ideal Day

There are many ways to get your life in balance. Creating a routine that is right for your lifestyle is a great way to do that. How many times do you find yourself saying at the end of the week, "I wish I had gotten this or that done," yet didn't get it done—again! Do you spend time each morning focusing on the ideals for the day? When you arrive at work, you probably open your e-mail and get caught up in all the minutiae. By the time you look up, the day is over and you feel like you got nothing accomplished. Is any of this ideal? Here are some ideas you can implement for a more empowering routine.

Author and speaker Brendon Burchard's opinion on e-mail is that it's about someone else's agenda, so don't spend your day engrossed in it. Schedule three or four times a day to review incoming e-mail. Instead of checking and responding at all times of the day, you are getting it done in chunks, which frees up your time to be creative and really productive.

What would an ideal day look like to you? Would you get lots accomplished, create happy clients, take good care of your staff, and have plenty of time for family and hobbies? Take some time now to create your ideal day on paper. When would you go to and leave work? How much time each day would you spend with your family? Would you work more or less? Would you have a regular routine in your daily life?

Time Blocking

Years ago in a seminar, I heard about time blocking and how to set up times when you seclude yourself from everyone and everything (which I touched on earlier). For most of my legal career, I've been setting aside time each day when I close out the world. I call this my "do not disturb" or "DND" time. That's when I focus intently on whatever I decide to put my attention on. Not having enough time in the day is caused by fragmentation, which DND time can help do away with. Whether it is a large project or a simple list of things I need to get done, my DND time is pure productivity. I have been able to get more done in an hour or two than most do all day. This method can be a game changer for you.

Time blocking has also really made a difference in my life. You block time in your calendar (on your computer, for instance) for working on projects or files that need attention. You can set up reminders that alert you when to work on your project. I block DND time for each day or week, depending on what my plans call for.

Your Rhythm

One day, a friend and I were talking about flow, balance, and life in general. He said it would behoove me to find a "rhythm" in my daily life. It was the best advice I had gotten in quite some time. I took a hard look at my day-to-day life and found new and better habits that I wanted to integrate into it. These included exercise, meditation, and time to focus on intentions and visualization.

Does your life flow upstream or down? Most of us live life as if we were paddling against the current, desperately trying to get where we want to be. Instead, why don't we get into the river and allow its current to carry us to our desired destination? When we resist life and are not creating our ideals, we find ourselves paddling upstream. But when we get into the mode of creating our ideals, we get into the downstream flow of life. Which way are you paddling?

Exploration:
- What are some things you would like to build into your daily plan?
- What new and empowering habits would you like to create?

My Ideal Day
- One hour of cardio (preferably a long walk outside with my dogs)
- At least thirty minutes of meditation
- Fifteen minutes visualizing my ideals
- Eating lighter foods such as green smoothies, salads, and vegetables (60 percent raw)
- Sharing of myself and making a difference in the world
- At least thirty minutes reading or listening to empowering and enlightening materials
- Living in the moment as much as possible
- At least two hours of undisturbed, productive creation time
- Seven or more hours of deep sleep at night

The Illusion of Control

> The only thing you can control in life is your reaction to it.
>
> —Unknown

Do you prefer uncertainty or certainty? I have learned that the only thing we can know for certain is that life is *not* certain. The more we attempt to be in control, the less we are. What would life be like if we were certain about everything? Some people live for uncertainty. They like to skydive or climb mountains to get the rush of not knowing what might come in the moment. Lawyers love certainty, so we do whatever possible to make sure of everything. Laws and rules are for making our lives as structured as possible.

However, attempting to control everything can lead to resistance and stress in our lives. If something does not line up with our expectations and preconceptions about what should happen, we experience a lot of irritation and judgment—which of course just leads to stress.

Life is all about change: it happens in nature every moment, all over the planet. Animals live in this constant state of change and uncertainty, which amounts to being in the moment. This means that living in the moment is "what is," and we will experience less stress by not resisting it. We must allow and accept both certainty and uncertainty.

10   The Ideal Life

9   Emotions

8   Balance

CHAPTER 16

As a nation, we ingest the most pharmaceuticals in the world per capita. We have some of the highest rates of alcoholism and drug addiction. Why? We have become a culture that refuses to feel emotions, pushing them down and ignoring them in the hope that they leave, never to return. Why do you think there are a million commercials for all that "anti"-depression medicine? Our society doesn't want to feel anything! Regardless of whether we use drugs, food, alcohol, the Internet, or something else to escape reality, it will always be there waiting for us. Emotions, and the physical feelings associated them, can't be ignored.

An emotion is just energy, a feeling we recognize in the body. (We could even think of the word as "e-motion"—energy in motion.) When you're happy, you have a feeling associated with it somewhere in your body. The same goes for every other emotion we create. When we try to suppress an emotion, it is still around, waiting. What is it waiting for? For release. You release emotion by experiencing it: feeling it!

Daily meditation helps release emotions that we've tried to ignore. Further, getting in the moment and experiencing our emotions as they come up means less stress on our bodies.

Exploration:

- How often during the day do you try to escape from your emotions and feelings?
- What do you end up doing the most? Mindless eating, Internet, television, or alcohol?
- What benefits have you received from these actions?
- Have they resulted in anything constructive in the long run?

Too many of us are not living our dreams, because we are living our fears.

—Les Brown

Exploration:

How can you experience your moment-to-moment emotions each day? Living in the present moment allows us to experience it all as it happens.

We usually head into resistance mode when we feel anything that we judge as bad or negative, so relaxing into the *feeling* of any emotion is the first step. You can then determine where the thought and emotion comes from in the subconscious, since our reactions are all based on past patterns and the perceptions filtered through our beliefs.

Next, figure out where in your body you feel the emotion. Is it in your head, neck, chest, or gut? Since emotion is just energy, when you actually feel the emotion in the moment, the energy can move on.

As Marianne Williamson said, "Your playing small does not serve the world." Is it time to fully experience your life by choosing to feel?

Healing

Through utter lack of integrity and greed, our profession has caused so much harm to so many, all over the world. Society has suffered dire consequences for the collective decisions of the law, governments, and lawyers. When *you* start to follow your heart's guidance and listen to your intuition, we can begin to heal these wounds. In addition, we all need *personal* healing due to the high level of stress in our profession.

What were the personal consequences to me of the stress of law school and my last fifteen years in the business? Here is the short list:

- Migraines that landed me in the hospital, as well as hundreds of tension headaches
- Irregular heartbeat (arrhythmia)
- Getting sick four or more times per year from being run-down and tired

Two years into the practice of law, I woke up one night around three a.m. and felt a weird sensation in my chest. I knew something was wrong with my heart; it clearly wasn't beating properly. Luckily, I wasn't having any chest pain, so I went to my doctor early the next morning. The next thing I knew, I was taken to the hospital and hooked up to a bunch of heart monitors. They diagnosed me with irregular heartbeat and sent me home with some medicine. In other words, the stress of law school sent me to the hospital with heart palpitations.

The doctors told me that I would have to be on medicine for this heart issue for the rest of my life. I didn't believe them; I knew it was all stress related. (I know that anything doctors say is just their opinion, and that they're doing the best they can based on their current level of consciousness.) Whenever I allowed myself to get stressed out, it would build until I created a migraine or irregular heartbeat.

The law also changed, and that had a profoundly negative impact on my personality. Before law school and the practice, I was fun, calm, relaxed, and enjoyable to be around. What I became scared me. Over the past twenty years, I developed the characteristics of being:

- Cynical
- Irritable
- Quick to anger
- Frequently on edge
- Always stressed
- Pessimistic
- Tensed up
- Always tired
- Resistant to dealing with other lawyers

How have you changed as a result of being in the legal profession? Think back to before law school. What were you like then? I became someone very different from the *real* me, and I set out to return. I have spent quite a bit of time meditating and releasing built-up emotions. This is the healing I needed to do to move on from all of it. Whether you stay in the practice of law or move on, it is important to allow yourself and your body to deeply heal the stress. It is time to be the real you again!

Exploration:

Close your eyes and ask yourself what in you needs to be released and healed. Any emotions that you feel as a result of these questions can be released quickly and easily by just *feeling* them.

- What walls have you put up that can be torn down now so you can return to your true self?
- What character traits have you taken on since you became a lawyer that you want to let go of?
- Who is the *real* you?

Creating a great daily routine with meditation, exercise, and incorporating more balance in my life was the solution to my issues. Quieting your mind is a powerful tool here. You end up giving your body space to relax and to release all the negativity. When your mind is constantly immersed in mind chatter, you are stuck there indefinitely.

The healing may take place quickly or over the span of several years, but keep with it. Allow yourself the time you need to get *you* back. When you allow yourself to heal, we all heal!

Life Is a Journey

You may have heard before that "life is a journey," but if I hear it over and over, it helps me keep in mind this very simple fact. Society and the ego want life to be about end results: how we will feel when this or that happens. You may hear self-talk like, "When I get ____, then I can feel happy!" or "When so and so does such and such, then things will change for me." But can we enjoy the now—as it is?

Buddhist traditions speak of this very principle over and over. The reason for suffering in life is the judgment we have in the moment. Accepting the paths we are on and then realizing we have the power to change them is powerful, but where we are right now is perfect too! All the lessons we have learned (or not) in our lives have made us who we are today. Ultimately, we can all learn how to better enjoy our individual journeys.

I can hear some of you asking, "Well, what about intentions? Aren't we focusing on the future when we visualize them?" Yes, you are consciously directing your attention to them in the moments of the day when you choose to do so. Having the faith, belief, and trust in the outcome at those times is the key. But when you're done with the visualizations, get back in the moment and live there as much as possible. Consciously create your intentions every day, let the path open up for you as it should, and let the universe figure out how to create the end result.

> We must rapidly begin the shift from a "thing-oriented" society to a "person-oriented" society.
>
> —Martin Luther King Jr.

PART FOUR

Be the Change

The Ideal Practice of Law
CHAPTER 17

The New Paradigm in the Profession

The legal profession has seen some drastic changes in the past ten or so years. The way we do business and how we offer our services to the public are much different from how they used to be. But the traditional ways of operating a law firm work exceptionally well: creating relationships and a referral network based on trust, time-honored business practices, and most important, integrity.

When we allowed our profession to be marketed through television commercials, radio, and billboards, the profession began down the slippery slope to becoming just a business. There is nothing per se wrong with personal injury law (or any other kind), but when those who practice it lack integrity and "create" cases, it costs us all a piece of the honor and trust our predecessors built up.

Practicing law begins with establishing trust. Trust is established when we do what we promise and do the right thing in each decision we make. When others know they can trust you, they go out of their way to send you business. When your business is built on these principles, you thrive. Many try to circumvent all this trust stuff and troll the public for business with flashy commercials. If you currently advertise for business, how can you reinvent your practice by building a law firm in the time-tested and honorable way?

Growing an Ideal Law Practice

Many times in this book I've mentioned doing business the way it used to be done: with honor and personal responsibility. For the most part, lawyers are very good technicians. What do I mean by that? Well, as a whole, we are usually very good at what we do: practicing law. But practicing law means you really run your own business, whether you're a solo practitioner or an associate at a law firm. Associates can become partners in a firm in a couple of different ways. They can bring in a good amount of business, or they can become assets that the firm doesn't want to lose to another (or to the associate's own new firm).

The business side of the law is what I've always loved. However, many practitioners today lack the business and entrepreneurial skills to set up and run a business as a referral machine. If you want to create an ideal business, whether it is a law firm, a consulting firm, being a writer, or following some other dream, learn business skills. They are universally applicable to anyone.

Video Lights the Way

No matter what area of practice you are in, teaching by video or audio is one of the most powerful ways anyone can market themselves in today's world. With video and audio, screencasts (or webcasts) and podcasts, you can share your expertise with your sphere of influence and ideal clients.

You can also set expectations for clients via video, educating them on the processes that they may go through as your client, or to explain standard features of a particular part of the legal system (such as family law). This saves you the time and energy of repeating the information yourself every time you take a case. It also builds trust and goes a long way to show you are an expert in your field (for instance, you can teach the ins and outs of conflict resolution if you practice litigation).

How have I used this idea to build my business? My ideal clients are real estate agents and mortgage lenders. I have recorded over thirty videos for educating real estate agents on contracts, the law, and marketing. I've also recorded videos for the end client, the home buyer. They explain the process of going to contract and the step-by-step process of closing title to property.

Video is the way people get their information today. Due to the vast amount of Internet video, people are spending more of their time on websites like YouTube and Facebook. With the Internet on our smartphones, tablets, and faster-than-ever home computers, video is here to stay!

What would have cost tens of thousands of dollars to create just a few years ago is now available to anyone with a computer, a decent thirty-dollar microphone, and some software (for instance, Camtasia or ScreenFlow are some options). With this inexpensive setup, you can record video of yourself, use a PowerPoint presentation, or just record audio. Setting up a channel for your business on YouTube is the easiest way to share your videos with others. (Did you know that it's the second-largest search engine nowadays?)

Let's say you have a new client who has the usual questions. Send a link to your Q&A video! Post such content on your website and add it to your social media outlets. Always be sure to include disclosures on your material as required by your local and state bars, plus whatever you feel is appropriate for the type of information you're providing. (And use your intuition when you do all of this.) These are only a few ideas with which you can add value for your clients. The more value you bring to the table, the more ideal clients will find you!

Websites are replacing many of the traditional attorney services. As you well know, much of what we do is form driven. People can do a last will and testament, set up a corporation, and get simple forms all online for much less than we would charge. The Internet will allow for more and more of this in the future. Yes, sometimes clients need advice and help, but many of our daily charge-for items are moving to the Internet. Further, video will begin to teach people how to complete these forms without the assistance of an attorney and at a much lower cost. Does this scare you? Why? If it scares you, then maybe you need to take a look at your beliefs!

Social media allows prospective clients to research you and check out what others say about you. If you aren't doing right by your clients, the news *will* make its way onto the Internet. This is the norm for all kinds of services and products today. Sites like angieslist.com give user reviews on household service providers. Social media, such as Facebook, Twitter, and LinkedIn can be used by angry clients to put the word out on lawyers they feel treated them wrongly. Anyone who is not operating their law practice with full integrity may have a hard time staying in business. The Internet has made the world a much smaller place.

We're also seeing alternative billing practices: the billable hour is on the way out, ladies and gents! Clients are seeking more predictable fee structures and want cases to be resolved in an efficient and timely way. A great article giving the Wisconsin Bar Association's honest thoughts on the profession and our future states very succinctly that the hourly fee structure is not dead, but that clients want attorneys to assume the risk of "keeping the meter running."†††††

Building a Sphere of Influence

Creating a network of contacts that know and trust you is a key component of building a successful law practice or business. Get out of your office and meet people who fit the description of good referral sources for you. Hone a list of what kinds of people meet these criteria. Where do your ideal referral sources spend their time? Where do they congregate? Go there and meet them. Don't forget to think beyond your local area; look online at groups on LinkedIn and other social networking sites. What do you do when you meet these ideal referral sources? How do you connect with them when they trust you enough? Some ideas are:

- Meet for coffee, breakfast, or lunch.
- Make a video that teaches them something.
- Create a blog with pertinent information for their industry.
- Create a monthly e-mail or snail-mail newsletter.
- E-mail them periodic updates on the law.
- Call them on the phone.
- Invite them to networking events you think they may benefit from.
- Forward them articles that they would be interested in (both personally and for business).

---

††††† This article was available from the Wisconsin Bar website when I first read it, but now it is for members only. Maybe the bar didn't want the public to see their findings? They are eye-opening! You can read the article here now: http:// www.reinhartlaw.com/Services/BusLaw/CorpGovern/Documents/ art1111%20TE.pdf

- Use greeting-card sender services.
- Create a series of autoresponder articles.
- Give workshops or seminars (and post recordings of them online).

Of course, after an in-person meeting, send a handwritten note and include a business card.

Networking

When I first got my law license, I wanted to find places to network where I could build referral sources. I tried just about everything: local chambers of commerce, networking groups, and private clubs.

The best decision I have made to date was to join the Tower Club in Fort Lauderdale. Even with my networking at all kinds of events, my business club was the real foundation on which I built my business. I attended functions at the club two or three times a week, and after about a year, people on my list of referral sources started to become my friends. Now, some of them are among my best friends, and I've been a club member for fifteen years. Just make a plan and get out there. Over time, you can deepen your current referral sources and add new ones.

Ideal Clients, Customers, and Team Members

An ideal business would not be complete without ideal clients, customers, and team members. Do you regularly attract ideal customers? Have you ever listed the characteristics of your ideal client?

When I used to visualize my ideal income, I found the money I wanted coming in, but a large percentage of my clientele was difficult to work with. I soon found the exact book to answer my question: "How do I attract the ideal client?" Stacey Hall and Jan Stringer's *Attracting Perfect Customers* came around at the perfect time. I was open to its ideas, which align with the principles "like attracts like" and "what you put your attention on grows."

Each quarter over the past five years, my team and I have reviewed our list of "perfect customer" characteristics, adding to or adjusting it as needed. This is the exact same procedure I have used to attract ideal team members into our business. After I determine what the ideal person(s) are like, I visualize them and feel the feeling of how amazing it is to have such ideal people in my life, as if they were already there.

Customer Service

Once you have attracted your ideal clients, it is time to wow them with amazing customer service. Meeting and connecting with ideal clients who also send you business is all well and good, but without the very best customer service, it is all for naught. To create "raving fans," team members should be trained that the customer is the lifeblood of the business and should be treated as such.

How can you empower employees to always do the very best they can for your customers, going the extra mile in *every* instance? How can you create culture in your firm that is rooted in amazing customer service?

Your Business Systems

Michael Gerber's books and his life's work inspired me to review everything we do in each type of transaction, down to the minutiae, so that any business can be systematized so that it has the possibility to run on autopilot with amazing customer service. Why? The main reason was that we wanted to be the best we could at every aspect of our law and title services.

Most day-to-day business processes can be broken down into action items. I believe you should review your business systems quarterly to improve them continually so that your team works smarter and offers the very best customer service possible.

Alternatives to Traditional Law Practice

Can we change the day-to-day practices of litigation and transaction work? Some enlightened ideas are changing the landscape. One I have come across recently is the paradigm represented by the International Academy of Collaborative Professionals. What they teach lawyers could transform not only family law, but also litigation and dispute resolution.

Their "collaborative" process of family law is a complete departure from the way things have been done for the past forty years. Instead of parties to a divorce paying large attorney fees fighting over minutiae, they agree to work together through an amicable dissolution process. The collaborative process is changing the lives not only of the attorneys who have integrated it into their practices, but the families who choose this route over the traditional court battle. I interviewed a divorce lawyer whose life (and clients' lives) have changed with this kind of practice. You can listen to it at http://www.Raisingthebarbook.com/interview1. The collaborative model can be used for any kind of dispute. I believe it is imperative that our profession embrace such enlightened pursuits of resolution. For more information, please see the IACP website (http://

collaborativepractice.com). The ABA Journal has written about the use of these principles also.‡‡‡‡‡

What can you do to revolutionize the way you practice law? Please share your ideas with our Facebook community.

Changes Coming to the Profession

> The attorney's role in society was once sacred. The attorney was a counselor, a confidant, and the most respected members in the community. Over time, the role of the lawyer has evolved, and societal changes, the economic downturn, and other factors have forced the attorney to view the practice of law less as profession and more as a business.
> —Wisconsin Bar Board of Governors§§§§§

What are the "other factors" the Wisconsin Bar believes have shaped the law profession in recent decades? In my opinion, it is an admission that there are too many lawyers. I know that no state or local bar associations *want* to admit this, since they are run and funded by their members, but this is the largest of our issues, aside from the changes in society. The Wisconsin Bar is spot on that we are a business and not a profession anymore. It is a buyer's market out there, and clients have more power to set up the fee structure they determine is in their own best interests.

Technological changes have also allowed small firms to compete with larger ones; this is partly because smaller firms can often integrate new tech much faster. The State Bar of Wisconsin's report also recommends that state and local bar associations share

---

‡‡‡‡‡http://www.abajournal.com/magazine/article/
integrative_law_puts_passion_into_the_profession/

§§§§§http://www.reinhartlaw.com/Services/BusLaw/CorpGovern/Documents/
art1111%20TE.pdf

responsibility for training new lawyers and setting up mentoring opportunities. The Internet also gives the layperson access to any statute, administrative code, or legal research for free. Many will educate themselves, and since what we normally "sell" to the public is information (and our opinion on how it applies to a client's situation), they can now create their own opinions.

The other massive change coming to the profession is the outsourcing of legal work. The Internet is chock full of articles discussing how more than one million lawyers in India and Asia are working for much less than their counterparts in America. Legal staffing companies are hiring attorneys who are licensed in your state to do what you're doing for much less than you charge.

Are you ready for all the coming changes? They are why you need recession- and downturn-proof business, and you build one on a sphere of influence. Further, when you change your limiting beliefs around money and business to *empowered* ones, you can thrive in any kind of economy.

Legal Education Needs Revamping

Our legal education system needs a major overhaul. A license to practice law in any state requires at least four years of undergraduate work, three years of law school, and a passing grade on its bar exam. In all of this education and testing, there is very little real-world instruction. (Granted, today there are slightly more internship and externship opportunities and a limited number of classes that try to include real-world experience.)

Common law shouldn't be as large a part of the curriculum as it is today. We need to teach law students how to practice law, starting in the first year. We should expand studies on how to run a law practice, as well as how to network and build a business traditionally.

I implore the powers that be to start these changes now and help future generations of lawyers to be better businesspeople who run their firms as consummate professionals with integrity. I will be a loud advocate for this from here on out. I hope you will be too!

The Need for Mentorship Programs

It is pretty evident that law graduates are struggling to find jobs in this marketplace. Many grads have given up and just hang a shingle with little or no real-world experience. When I was a new grad contemplating what I might do with my future, I considered opening my own firm. I went as far as buying a few books and outlining my business plan! As any experienced lawyer will tell you, unless a grad works with an attorney in their desired area(s) of practice, there is too much to know to "just hang a shingle." Who really pays the price for the lack of postgraduate real-world experience? The clients are impacted the most (followed by those of us in the practice).

In my opinion, this issue is as pervasive a problem as any right now. I have some compassion for these graduates, since they often have no choice if they want to stay in the business. With the lack of jobs and the student loan payments that can be put off for only so long, what are they to do? Mentorship programs can help. I live in Broward County in South Florida, which has a mentorship program in effect. It seems to be gaining some traction in my community. Such programs can model a new system for assisting graduates. There is a real need for experienced attorneys to share with and help our new bar members. We need local bar associations to create the programs (the state bars can help in smaller counties).

I was lucky enough to have a mentor in my previous law partner when I was new. Luckily, I didn't make the mistake of trying to go it on my own. Inexperienced attorneys don't know what they don't know, and it *is* scary—for us and them. Are you an experienced lawyer who could mentor a youngster and make our profession a better place? See if your local bar has a mentorship program and get involved. If it doesn't, get one started!

Attorney Regulation and Oversight

Would you agree that lawyers regulating and overseeing other lawyers is an inherent conflict of interest? Isn't this asking the fox to guard the henhouse? It is hard to believe that we "police" our own. Most professions have outside bodies and government agencies that regulate its membership through license law. I know in Florida that we have licensed attorneys who decide the fates of other attorneys. Some would say that this is acceptable, since who other than attorneys know better how to deal with misconduct?

Attorneys, who make up the majority of legislatures, make the laws. They are also among the lobbyists for and against said laws, the only citizens allowed to be part of the judiciary, and many of the presidents were lawyers. See where I'm going with this? We have a stranglehold on this country in so many ways. This needs to change!

What ideas do you have? How can you be part of this change for the better?

Masterminding

CHAPTER 18

The Power of Small Groups

> Never doubt that a small group of thoughtful, committed citizens can change the world. Indeed, it's the only thing that ever has.
>
> —Margaret Mead

What the Bleep Do We Know!? describes an interesting 1993 experiment done in Washington, DC. From June 7 until July 30, 1993, four thousand people participated in a meditation project. The intention behind it was to see if a group of meditators alone could drop the level of violent crimes in the city. The group had started at twenty-five hundred. They predicted a 20 percent drop in crime, but the drop was 25 percent. Local police departments participated by collecting and analyzing the information (and even contributed to the published paper).****** Many other studies have since created similar results.

Skeptics will doubt a person's or small group's ability to shift mass consciousness, but I challenge them to look at their own beliefs and see if their lives change when they change their beliefs. I've seen it work time and time again in my own life. I've uncovered

---

****** http://www.istpp.org/crime_prevention/

deep, long-held limiting beliefs and replaced them with better ones. My life changed dramatically!

In Napoleon Hill's 1930s classic book, *Think and Grow Rich*, he spoke about gaining power through the use of the "mastermind," as he called it. I read it while I was in college and have reread it many times. At one point, the material on small groups hit me and I decided to create one. Over the years, I've facilitated and participated in many mastermind groups.

So what exactly is a mastermind group? Hill defines it as "coordination of knowledge and effort, in a spirit of harmony, between two or more people, for the attainment of a definite purpose." I've also seen it defined in several other books as two or more people coming together with a common purpose and desire to support each other with ideas, encouragement, insights, and resources in a noncompetitive environment.

As companion to this book, I've created a mastermind group framework for attorneys. Some benefits of full-out participation will include:

1. Hearing others' ideas on personal growth, marketing, business strategies, personal and business relationships, networking, health and fitness, life balance, career growth, opportunities, and a multitude of other topics
2. Gaining opportunities for business referrals and increased income
3. Receiving feedback on projects or ideas
4. Learning about new systems and technology available to the legal profession
5. Being a part of the change you wish to see in the profession

As Mr. Hill said, you will "accomplish more in a year than you would on your own in a lifetime without the group." Mr. Hill gave two overriding principles of mastermind groups. The first is a tangible benefit from being involved in one: the economic advantage from being around and partnered with other like-minded professionals. In my opinion, though, the deeper and more powerful principle is "tapping into the universal mind—intelligence beyond yourself." In other words, when we are interconnected within a small group, members can tap into the universal mind where all ideas exist.

What are some other small groups that have impacted consciousness and our world? This country was founded by a small group that was largely made up of well-respected lawyers. Did you know that thirty-two of the fifty-five framers of the Constitution were lawyers? Thomas Jefferson and John Adams had a massive impact on the early government of our country, and both were attorneys. Apple Computer was once a small group with a clear vision for its industry. Jesus and his disciples were a small group that had a massive impact on the world, and so were Buddha and his followers.

What about Moses, Lao Tzu, and many of the other enlightened teachers who have graced this planet? They all led small groups that made a difference. Benjamin Franklin also headed up a mastermind group that he called "the Junto" and wrote frequently about its exchange of ideas and benefits to its members. Gandhi brought the British government to its knees without a single gun using consciousness and awareness and what started out as a small group, gaining India's independence from the dominant world power of the British Empire.

Will you be a trailblazer? Be the first in your community to set up a mastermind group to start shifts in yourself and in others. I've started the ball rolling, using my own expertise and background as a facilitator and member of such groups. My new group is intended to be nationwide and to allow members to tap into the resources of the whole group as things progress. At some point, we will take it worldwide.

What would it be like to be a part of this empowered and amazing group of lawyers who want to change themselves and the profession? Don't wait. Be a part of the change you wish to see: visit www.EsquireMM.com.

When you sign up for more information, you'll get access to several videos exploring the concept. They'll teach you about consciousness and building a business based in integrity. *Be the change; lead the change!*

10 The Ideal Life

Emotions

CHAPTER 19

The future does not belong to those who are content with today, apathetic toward common problems and their fellow man alike, timid and fearful in the face of bold projects and new ideas. Rather, it will belong to those who can blend passion, reason and courage in a personal commitment to [their] ideals.

—Robert F. Kennedy

Society suffers from a severe case of apathy, and it has for some time. People just don't seem to care about anything but themselves. Human beings tend to be apathetic toward things that don't directly affect their own lives. You clearly are different, aren't you? If you've read this far, then you have a desire for something more—to grow and to connect with the infinite possibilities contained in the intentions you will create.

Without a clear vision, human beings perish. Each of us, and our profession as a whole, needs a clear and powerful vision for the future. I have my own vision for what I want our profession to look like. This vision will expand and grow as time passes and our mastermind group hones and clarifies it.

Exploration:

- What has stopped you from changing your habits and behaviors in the past?
- What have you had apathy toward?
- What do you want our profession to *really* be like?
- What is your vision for your personal and professional life? What qualities and characteristics does your ideal life hold in your vision?

My Vision of the Ideal

Attorneys are problem solvers, not problem creators. We work toward the common good, helping our clients to resolve issues they cannot solve themselves. Lawyers make decisions based on our hearts and intuition; we always know the right thing to do, and we do it. We have balance in our lives, both personal and professional. We are deeply aware of how each decision affects the whole: us and society, and this ideal guides each and every decision we make. Society sees us in a different light as we earn back the respect the profession once had. Our every action is with complete integrity and honor. Those in the dark are shown the path of possibilities. The law becomes an honorable and respected profession once again.

The best way to remake the world is by starting with yourself and your own internal world.

—Thom Hartmann,
The Last Hours of Ancient Sunlight

Did this book "awaken" you to some new and empowering ideas? Allow its information and ideas to be your alarm clock. Allow the framework for change to create the new you, and we will change the profession. You create your reality; therefore, you have immense power to create your ideal life. Through this power and by joining together with other like-minded lawyers who have the same vision and want to grow, we will shift consciousness for the better.

> To put the world right in order, we must first put the nation in order; to put the nation in order, we must first put the family in order; to put the family in order, we must first cultivate our personal life; we must first set our hearts right.
>
> —Confucius

If you died tomorrow, what would your life have meant? Could you say that you had a positive impact on the world? What would people say about you at your funeral? You have a real opportunity to make your mark on this planet, and the way to do so is to live with integrity in all you do. To wake up and begin to create your reality, not based on someone else's beliefs but on what you choose to believe from here on out. Are you willing to take full-on responsibility for what you create from now on?

Regardless of whether you decide to stay in the profession and make it a better place or you feel you'll find your life's purpose elsewhere, it is a great idea to integrate into your life the principles you feel are needed. I outline some possibilities below.

- Live life in the moment.
- Release old, limiting beliefs and create new and empowered beliefs.
- Live from your heart space and intuition.
- Acknowledge your life's purpose and move toward it every day.
- Quiet your mind through meditation.
- Heal your mind and body from the stress of the profession.
- Get clear on ideals in every area of your life.
- Visualize and feel your ideals as *complete*, every day.
- Have faith, trust, and belief.
- Give up control of outcomes and attachments.
- Wake up to an aware and conscious life where you *create your reality*.
- Live your life with complete and unwavering honor and integrity.

This may seem like a long list, but in reality, this is pretty simple stuff. If you integrate these things into your life, all the while learning more about them and living them, it all becomes second nature. The Japanese principle of *kaizen* entails making small improvements every day, which, after a while, creates massive change. When we make better choices every day, whether it be to eat healthier or to do the right thing for anyone we meet, after months and years, you really do make a difference.

Take a look at our society today. What if more and more people started to make heart-based decisions in their lives? What would the world be like? It would be a whole lot different. We would actually take care of one another and live as we really are: interconnected.

You don't need to implement the entire framework all at once. Start with small steps, and you will find tremendous change in yourself soon.

Your time has come to thrive and create your ideal life! Your intuition guided you to this book. You know that the profession needs to change, but you didn't know how or if it was even possible. As I have shown, this change begins with you! Life begins to open up when you do. It is up to *all* of us to create this new vision for our profession. Every decision we make impacts the whole, so be aware as you make each and every choice.

The future depends on what you do today.

—Gandhi

The world is before you, and you need not take it or leave it as it was when you came in.

—James Baldwin

To all the nonlawyers who have read this book: start a movement for a return to integrity in your own profession. Every profession is plagued with greed and a lack of honesty. The framework for the integrity movement is ready for you to implement. Write, speak, and help implement some solutions to the challenges in your profession. Each and every one of us makes a difference, and when other professions connect with this movement, we all win.

When you really look at what our lives truly are, you'll see that they are very simply just one experience after the next. In each experience and moment, we have free will to decide how we would like our lives to be. We have the choice to decide to live with integrity in all we do, or to ignore the little voices in our hearts that tell us what the right thing is. If you listen to that little voice and do the right thing, we all benefit. One moment and one decision at a time. That's how we got where we are—one decision at a time—and it will be how we create our future.

I implore you to look into the suggested readings and join our mastermind group. Attend some workshops and enlighten yourself. Read some books and grow. Get in the moment and listen to your intuition, and our profession will be honorable once again.

Did this book make a difference for you? If so, we want to hear from you! Visit our Facebook site at www.Facebook.com/RaisingTheBarBook.

If you know anyone who might benefit from this work, then please do them a favor and share it with them. This work is about the message. The more of us who awaken, the ever closer we come to our ideal legal profession.

> Do your little bit of good where you are; it's those little bits of good that overwhelm the world!
>
> —Desmond Tutu

Together we can do anything, including change the world! I look forward to seeing you at one of my seminars someday and having you join us at the mastermind group in your local area.

Here's to creating your ideal reality,

Adam J. Ouellette, Esq

For a printable list of all the exercises in this book, please see www.raisingthebarbook.com/exercises.

Resources

Take action NOW. Join our movement!

Mastermind group information: www.EsquireMM.com

Join us at live seminars:
www.EsquireAcademy.com

The latest, updated list of resources is at:
www.RaisingTheBarBook.com/thelist

Books

Tolle, Eckhart. *The Power of Now: A Guide to Spiritual Enlightenment*

This was the first book I read on anything to do with the present moment. It is a definite must read, as are Tolle's other books.

Brown, Michael. *The Presence Process: A Healing Journey into Present Moment Awareness*

This book takes up where Tolle's book ends, with exercises and a framework on how to live your life in the moment.

Childre, Doc and Howard Martin. *The HeartMath Solution: The Institute of HeartMath's Revolutionary Program for Engaging the Power of the Heart's Intelligence*

Buzan, Tony. *The Mind Map Book: How to Use Radiant Thinking to Maximize Your Brain's Untapped Potential*

Chopra, Deepak. *The Book of Secrets: Unlocking the Hidden Dimensions of Your Life*

The Spontaneous Fulfillment of Desire: Harnessing the Infinite Power of Coincidence to Create Miracles

Gandhi, Mohandas K. *Autobiography: The Story of My Experiments with Truth*

Howard, Philip K. *Life Without Lawyers: Restoring Responsibility in America*

Hendricks, Gay. *The Big Leap: Conquer Your Hidden Fear and Take Life to the Next Level*

Conscious Living: Finding Joy in the Real World

Braden, Gregg. *The Spontaneous Healing of Belief: Shattering the Paradigm of False Limits*

The Divine Matrix: Bridging Time, Space, Miracles, and Belief

McTaggart, Lynne. *The Intention Experiment: Using Your Thoughts to Change Your Life and the World*

Assaraf, John and Murray Smith. *The Answer: Grow Any Business, Achieve Financial Freedom, and Live an Extraordinary Life*

Allen, David. *Getting Things Done: The Art of Stress-Free Productivity*

Trapani, Gina. *Lifehacker: 88 Tech Tricks to Turbocharge Your Day*

Simmons, Gary. *The I of the Storm: Embracing Conflict, Creating Peace*

Gawain, Shakti. *Creative Visualization: Use the Power of Your Imagination to Create What You Want in Your Life*

Allen, James. *As a Man Thinketh*

Finley, Guy. *The Secret of Letting Go*

Pink, Daniel H. *Drive: The Surprising Truth About What Motivates Us*

Hill, Napoleon. *Think and Grow Rich*

Keeva, Steven. *Transforming Practices: Finding Joy and Satisfaction in the Legal Life*

Brach, Tara. *Radical Acceptance: Embracing Your Life with the Heart of a Buddha*

Peirce, Penney. *The Intuitive Way: The Definitive Guide to Increasing Your Awareness*

Hartmann, Thom. *The Last Hours of Ancient Sunlight (Revised and Updated): The Fate of the World and What We Can Do Before It's Too Late*

Burchard, Brendon. *The Charge: Activating the 10 Human Drives That Make You Feel Alive*

Kierson, Miles. *Seven Provocations: A Novel About One Man's Spiritual Awakening*

Inghilleri, Leonardo and Micah Solomon. *Exceptional Service, Exceptional Profit: The Secrets of Building a Five-Star Customer Service Organization*

Performance Research Associates. *Delivering Knock Your Socks Off Service*

Mitchell, Jack. *Hug Your Customers: The Proven Way to Personalize Sales and Achieve Astounding Results*

Burg, Bob and John David Mann. *The Go-Giver: A Little Story About a Powerful Business Idea*

Brodie, Richard. *Virus of the Mind: The New Science of the Meme*

Adrienne, Carol. *The Purpose of Your Life: Finding Your Place in the World Using Synchronicity, Intuition, and Uncommon Sense*

Attwood, Chris and Janet. *The Passion Test: The Effortless Path to Discovering Your Life Purpose*

Millman, Dan. *The Life You Were Born to Live: A Guide to Finding Your Life Purpose*

Jantsch, John. *The Referral Engine: Teaching Your Business to Market Itself*

Duct Tape Marketing (Revised and Updated): The World's Most Practical Small Business Marketing Guide

Gerber, Michael E., Robert Armstrong, and Sanford Fisch. *The E-Myth Attorney: Why Most Legal Practices Don't Work and What to Do About It*

Films

What the Bleep Do We Know?!

Gandhi

Peaceful Warrior

> The story of Dan Millman's life. A great book to read as well.

Beyond Belief

> A documentary about beliefs and how they create your reality.

Finding Joe

> A documentary about the teacher and writer Joseph Campbell, who spent his life exploring human mythos. He was a visionary and an amazing teacher.

Articles

Trafton, Anne. "The Benefits of Meditation"

Software, Productivity, and Apps

iMindMap: www.thinkbuzan.com

Evernote: http://www.Evernote.com

OmniFocus: www.omnigroup.com

> Great for projects and planning, even everyday to-do lists. For Mac and iOS.

Planner Pads: www.Plannerpads.com

> The best paper planner I have ever found, and I have tried them all.

Camtasia: www.techsmith.com

If you happen to purchase anything I recommend in this or any of my communications, I may receive some kind of affiliate compensation. I only recommend books that I have read and other materials I use in my life and business. If there is ever an issue with anything I recommend, please alert me.

An Open Letter to Anyone Considering Law School:

If you are on the fence about law school, I would like to offer a couple of suggestions.

Talk with someone who already works in the area of practice you are drawn to. Make a list of items you would like to know about. Find out what their normal day is like, what they spend most of their time on, and so on. I have sat with many prospective students and recent grads who wanted to know about what we do, and I'll be doing this even more often now.

If you are in college, get a part-time job at an attorney's office; intern without pay if need be. See what it is all about and judge for yourself if this is the career choice for you. Quite a few of my friends from law school did this as a full-time job before they even enrolled, so they knew it was the right choice going in. My concern is for students who are either on the fence or have no idea if the law is the right fit and just blindly go into it without some background investigation.

Check out the preference test at the 14-Point Law School Quotient Quiz.[††††††]

Use the framework I outline in this book (or read a few books). If all signs point to yes, then you can move forward, but look at all your options. There are plenty of current and prospective attorneys who *do* have the calling and are right for the profession, but there are many more who get into it without doing their homework and create miserable existences for themselves. Your *heart,* not your head, will give you a clear signal if this is the right decision for your life. Look beyond the choice of law as your career. If everyone who considered

---

[††††††] http://www.nisiprius.com/lawschoolquiz.php

the law really thought it through, we would have far fewer attorneys and a decidedly different profession.

Disclaimer

The Publisher has strived to be as accurate and complete as possible in the creation of this guide, notwithstanding the fact that he does not warrant or represent at any time that the contents within are accurate due to the rapidly changing nature of the Internet and other rapidly changing programs that are used for publishing.

While all attempts have been made to verify information provided in this publication, the Publisher assumes no responsibility for errors, omissions, or contrary interpretation of the subject matter herein. Any perceived slights of specific persons, peoples, or organizations are unintentional. Any registered trademarks are property of their respective owners.

In practical advice books, like anything else in life, there is no guarantee of income made. Readers are cautioned to rely on their own judgment about their individual circumstances to act accordingly.

This book is not intended for use as a source of medical, legal, business, accounting, or financial advice. All readers are advised to seek services of competent professionals in the fields of medicine, law, business, accounting, and finance.